Love and Logic Magic for Early Childhood

Practical Parenting from Birth to Six Years

The Love and Logic
PRESS Inc.
www.loveandlogic.com

Jim Fay & Charles Fay, Ph.D.

First edition
Second printing, 2000
Printed in the United States of America

ISBN 1-930429-00-2

Library of Congress Card Number: 00-101452

Book Production and Design
Publication Coordinator: Charles Fay, Ph.D., Golden, CO
Editor: Adryan Russ, Glendale, CA
Copyediting: Linda Carlson, Erie, CO
Cover & Book Design: Bob Schram/Bookends, Boulder, CO
Illustration: John Martin
Project Coordinator: Carol Thomas

Table of Contents

Also authored by Jim Fay

Helicopters, Drill Sergeants and Consultants
Trouble-Free Teens
Pearls of Love and Logic for Parents and Teachers
Teaching with Love and Logic

(with Charles Fay, Ph.D.)

Teacher in Charge
Calming the Chaos

Jim Fay and Charles Fay, Ph.D. are also regular contributors
to the Love and Logic Journal

Order our complete catalog of
stress-free parenting and teaching titles:
1-800-338-4065
or visit our website:
www.loveandlogic.com

Acknowledgements

Jim, Foster, and Little Charlie

Cancun, Mexico, 1978. Foster Cline, future world-renowned child psychiatrist, and I sat in the cabana on the beach. Foster was and still is my very best friend, loyal partner, and personal guru. We had guided 120 teachers and parents to the resort for three weeks of fun and study. Most of the participants were rollicking in the surf while Foster and I were chasing our passion. The flame behind that passion, known as Love and Logic®, has not dwindled one bit over the years that have passed since that day.

Foster and I were designing yet another lesson for our students. The energy was evident as we threw ideas at each other at warp speed. This is what happens every time we get together.

"We have to make this even more practical and easier to master than the last lesson," enthused Foster. "That way they'll remember the technique and use it as soon as they see their kids again."

Make it simple. Make it easy to remember. And best of all, make it practical. Those have been the watchwords of our teaching from day one. Over the years these principles have not only attracted millions to study Love and Logic, but have captured Foster's and my imaginations and energies.

Little did we know, on that day, a 14-year-old boy was watching us. This boy was Charlie Fay, my son. He was curious about why his dad and Foster had so much fun working together. Not only was he curious, he was determined to find out. So this was not the only time that he stayed close and eavesdropped on our every word. This is why he often appeared in the back of the classroom when Foster and I were teaching together.

It was years later, that Charlie explained to us why he had studied to become a psychologist. "I watched the two of you share the joys of your friendship and teaching. I watched your enthusiasm as your first books and training programs became realities. I came to realize that what you did was not work. It was play. It was a passion. It was never a job."

Charlie continued, "Dad. I watched you and Mom setting up businesses. You worked together at the dining room table, licking stamps, making flyers, helping parents and teachers on the phone, counting advertising pieces, and stapling books. Even that wasn't a job for you. It was passion.

"I decided that when I grew up I was going to be part of your dream to make Love and Logic a household word. I just never let you know it."

Once I heard Charlie talk about this I knew why he had become such an outstanding psychologist, writer, and speaker. Not only did he earn a Ph.D. in school psychology, but also he had been studying Love and Logic with Foster and me since he was a child.

That 14-year-old boy who eavesdropped on Foster and me back in the nineteen seventies is now a valued consultant to me in my work. He serves along with Foster W. Cline, M.D., as a valued resource and partner in the continued study and evolution of the Love and Logic philosophy.

The direction and inspiration for this book, *Love and Logic Magic for Early Childhood*, comes from Charles W. Fay, Ph.D. His creativity and exceptional writing skill is evident throughout the book. I cannot tell you how proud I am to be part of the book.

And how excited I am to offer more creative Love and Logic solutions for parents of young children through this book, *Love and Logic Magic for Early Childhood.*

If you have as much fun and get as many rewards from reading this book as we did creating and producing it, we will all have a winner on our hands.

Jim Fay

Preface

How would it be if you could giggle your way through a book and also gain time-tested, powerful tools for raising happy, responsible kids? Wouldn't it be great if this very same book had so many fun techniques and examples that it actually started making you look forward to your young children misbehaving? Wouldn't it be wonderful if these very same tools and techniques could lower your stress level during these challenging years? These were just a few of the dreams we lived by as we sat writing this book at our computers.

"Let's make this book really fun to read with lots of practical examples," I (Charles) said to my dad.

"Great! And let's be sure to give a bunch of solutions for really common problems people have with their young children . . . frustrating things they deal with each and every day," he replied.

What problems are the most typical and challenging for parents of young children? We both sat down, asked each other this question, and made a list. It read something like this:

- Grocery store temper tantrums
- Bedtime battles
- Power struggles over eating
- Getting them to brush their teeth
- Potty training

- Whining and saying things like, "Not fair!" or, "But why?"
- Kids who won't get ready on time in the mornings
- Sibling rivalry
- Getting them to pick up their toys
- Temper tantrums and fits in the restaurant
- When they say, "No!" all of the time
- Begging for toys or candy in the check-out line
- Misbehaving at day care, preschool, or kindergarten

The more items we added to the list, the more excited we became about writing this book! Why are we so excited about young children and their misbehavior?

First, our great joy and enthusiasm grows more and more each day as we hear success story after success story, describing how parents of young children have used Love and Logic to bring the fun back into parenting.

Secondly, we've also seen how important the first six years of life are. When parents start using Love and Logic early in their children's lives, they often say things like, "I didn't think parenting could be this much fun!" When parents wait too long to start, instead they say, "I wish I had started this stuff a whole lot earlier. Now things are really a battle."

Thirdly, we love it when kids misbehave and make mistakes around Love and Logic adults. Why? Because Love and Logic teaches how to turn every mistake your child makes into a golden nugget of wisdom. The more mistakes your children make, the wiser they can become!

Are you ready to have some fun?
If so, read on!

About the Authors

JIM FAY'S background includes thirty-one years as a teacher and administrator, fifteen years as a professional consultant and public speaker, and many years as a parent of three children.

He serves both nationally and internationally as a consultant to schools, parent organizations, counselors, mental health organizations, and the U.S. military.

Jim believes his major accomplishment in life is the development of a unique philosophy (along with Foster W. Cline, M.D.) of practical techniques for enhancing communication between children and adults, known as Love and Logic. Jim has taken complex problems and broken them down into simple, easy-to-use concepts and techniques that can be understood and used by anyone. Hundreds of thousands of people have expressed how Love and Logic has enhanced their relationships with their children.

Jim is one of America's most sought after presenters in the area of parenting and school discipline. His practical techniques are revolutionizing the way parents and professionals are looking at how we deal with children, how we help them become responsible, thinking people, and how we help them enhance their own self-concepts.

DR. CHARLES FAY is a parent, Nationally Certified School Psychologist, and consultant to schools, parent groups, and mental health professionals across the United States. His expertise in developing and teaching practical discipline and behavior management strategies has been refined through work with severely disturbed children and adolescents in school, hospital, and community settings. His interest in this field resulted from years of watching and learning from two internationally recognized experts . . . his father, Jim Fay, and their friend Foster Cline, M.D. Charles crafts each of his presentations with care, packing them with stories, examples, laughs, and lots of practical solutions.

Dr. Charles Fay received his Ph.D. with highest honors from the University of South Carolina School Psychology Program, a psychologist training program recognized as one of the most competitive and rigorous in the United States. Dr. Fay has also earned national certification from the National Association of School Psychologists (NASP).

Charles has now taken an active role in blending his unique psychological background and expertise with the Love and Logic techniques originally developed by his father and Dr. Cline. Throughout the United States, Charles has received high praise for his presentations.

CHAPTER ONE

Basic Ingredients of "Love and Logic" Magic

Parenting Can Be a Joy!

Imagine yourself sitting at the dining room table. Guests are gathered around the table for an early Sunday dinner, and you have every hope that your two-year-old is not going to become a demon. While everyone is enjoying food and conversation, he waddles over to the staircase he knows is clearly off-limits. Why do young kids pick times when their parents have company to attempt a little toddler terrorism?

He gets that dreaded look on his face that almost says, "Get your army together, prepare for battle, let's get it on!" He heads for the stairs. You say to him, firmly but kindly, "No, Sweetie. I'll take you upstairs after we finish dinner." In your heart, you want to believe that a child—this child—can learn to listen the first time. In your soul, you desperately want to believe that this new stuff called Love and Logic will really work.

You see him on the second stair, which he's just climbed. You decide to try what you read in the book. You smile at him and sing, "Uh-oh. Uh-oh." You pick him up, bring him to the table and hold him lovingly. Following the book's instructions, you add softly, "Sit beside me, Honey, on the floor—here between my legs—while I eat."

Now, Junior is not thanking you for your new parenting technique. He is throwing a fit. You look down at him, smile, and simply say, "How sad. You can come up when you're acting sweet."

He throws an even bigger fit. An adult at the table says, "He's only a little child." Another says, "You're being too hard." You politely ask those adults if they would like to have dinner in the garage. There's a moment of awkward silence; then someone changes the subject. Everyone ignores Junior, and you begin to silently pray.

After a few minutes, your little sweetie is no longer whining or crying. "Maybe it will work!" you say to yourself. Now that he's calm, you excuse him from sitting under your feet. Free at last, he heads straight back to the stairs. All conversation stops, and your guests' mouths hang open.

He looks at the stairs, back at you, then at the stairs, then back at you. "Uh-oh," you sing once more. Finally, he points to the forbidden second stair and says to himself, "Uh-oh. No!" Then, to the amazement of everyone at the table, he sits on the first stair and smiles sweetly at you.

Oh, the love and confidence you see on his face! This, you tell yourself, is how happy kids look when they have the security of knowing where the limits are and that their parents are not going to lose control to maintain them.

❤ ❤ ❤

Wouldn't it be great if you could sing "Uh-oh" to your children—just two syllables—and, like Junior, they would stop in their tracks? Would you consider it a miracle if, with a single phrase like "Uh-oh," your children would mind you? Wouldn't it be great if you never had to raise your voice again in frustration and anger?

You're thinking, yes, yes, yes, in answer to all these questions and wondering what on earth you have to do to make the dream come true. We're not going to tell you to love your kids more. You've already proven that you love them by taking the time to read this book. What we are going to do is give you some practical strategies for raising them without raising your blood pressure.

> **With Love and Logic, your children will learn how to live with the consequences of their actions, avoid blaming others for their problems, and make wise decisions.**

What you're about to read requires an investment—of time and practice—but it will repay you and your children for generations to come.

The "Las Vegas" Plan

The story you just read about the toddler on the stairs is not a fairy tale. It really did happen, and it can happen in your house, too. For more than 25 years now, parents have been telling us: "It really works! Love and Logic ideas are easy. They're also so much fun that I actually look forward to my kids misbehaving, so I can use them!"

There are never any guarantees in parenting. Raising kids is tougher than ever. Like pulling the lever on a Las Vegas slot machine, you give it your best tug and hope for the best. What Love and Logic can promise is to raise the odds of children turning out well, especially when parents start early. We're excited about this book. We believe that by using its principles now, you make a great investment in your children's future.

Investing in the Future

People who move from one day to the next, without thinking about the days and years to come, wind up unprepared for the future. Remember the story, "The Grasshopper and the Ant"?

One winter day, an ant was busy working with its fellow ants to dry their stored supply of corn, which had gotten damp during a rainstorm. A grasshopper approached and begged the ant to spare her a few grains. "I'm starving," the grasshopper said.

Even though it was against his principle to stop working, one ant stopped for a moment and asked, "May I ask what you were doing all last spring and summer? Why didn't you collect a store of food for the winter?"

"The fact is," replied the grasshopper, "I was busy singing. I didn't have time."

"If you spent the summer singing," said the ant, "you're going to have to spend the winter dancing." And he went back to work.

Not a very charitable ant? Perhaps. But he was right to question the grasshopper's failure to think about his future. Do you suppose it's wise to invest early, in the "spring" of our children's lives, so that we don't have to spend the winter dancing around teenagers who are out of control? We are guessing that you already know this. That's why you're reading this book.

Let's take a look at Tess, a 15-year-old whose parents—unlike you—didn't start early.

"This is a stupid dinner, and I refuse to eat it!" said Tess to her mother.

"I've just spent two hours making it, and you're going to eat it!" her mother retorted. "You'll eat this dinner, or you'll eat nothing!"

"Oh, now you're going to starve me!" Tess said. "What are you going to do, put a lock on the refrigerator? I'm going down to Robby's Cafe and eat what I want!" she said, getting up from the table and grabbing a jacket out of the hall closet.

Tess walked out the door and slammed it shut.

Now, let's look at what you can look forward to by investing early.

"Greg," his mother said with concern. "You're picking at your food. Aren't you hungry?"

"I'm sorry, Mom," 16-year-old Greg said quietly, "I didn't do well on my math test today, and it looks like my grade's going down. I just don't feel like eating."

"What a bummer," his mother said. "Want me to save you a plate for later?"

"Thanks. May I be excused? I guess I should go look at my math homework and try to make some sense out of it."

❤ ❤ ❤

Greg's mother started early, making deposits into her parenting account. We thank *you* for starting early too! Down the road, there will be lots of other people who'll thank you, too—your child's teachers, friends, loved ones—and, in about ten or twenty years—your child.

Four Types of Deposits: The Basic Principles of Love and Logic

Are children ingesting far more information than we did at their age? Is some of this information very positive and healthy? Is some of it, by contrast, very scary? Clearly, kids are facing far more serious—sometimes life-and-death—decisions than ever before. Are they going to need more wisdom than we did, just to survive? Where are they going to get this wisdom? Here's the good news:

Regardless of all our technological advances, parents will always be the most important source of information and values for their growing children.

How can parents provide this essential information? By using the four basic Love and Logic ingredients. What do these ingredients offer? They give parents a practical investment strategy for building their children's self-esteem, personal responsibility, and ability to make smart choices. Wise people like you start early in their children's lives, making four types of deposits. Through their everyday lives with their children, they try their best to:

- Build the self-concept
- Share the control or decision-making
- Offer empathy, then consequences
- Share the thinking and problem-solving

PRINCIPLE #1: *Build the Self-Concept*

Self-concept is our road map for life. It determines where we go and how we get there. Will we experience dirt roads with lots of ruts or paved highways that make our journey smooth? Will our self-concept be high, or will it be low, and what determines the difference?

Some parents guess that a child with a high self-concept has attained it by living in a family with lofty ideals or an expensive lifestyle and that a child with a low self-concept must have been battered or abused. In fact, the building of both the high and the low self-concept happen over time, to all kinds of families, and both are based on small "deposits" that are made on a daily basis—one piece of information at a time. Take a look at Aida.

"No!" Aida's mother said with exasperation. "How many times must I tell you how to put on your clothes?" she shouted.

Little Aida looked up at her mother, her smile turning to a frown, and said, "I like to put on my socks first."

"It's just not right," her mother said, more calmly. "You put on your dress first. Then, you put on your socks and shoes. Here, I'll do it for you. Come over here, right now."

"My feet are cold, so I put on my socks first," the six-year-old told her mother.

"I don't have time for this foolishness," her mom said, looking at her watch, dressing her child. "You never listen, and you never do things the way you're supposed to do them. What am I going to do with you?"

❤ ❤ ❤

Every time Aida is treated this way constitutes a "withdrawal" from her healthy self-concept account. Despite the fact that her mother would probably be the last person to wish a low self-concept on her daughter, she is, unwittingly, helping to create it.

At Alec's house, things are different.

"Alec, honey!" his mother said, "You still have your slippers on and we have to go to school. The car leaves in five minutes."

"I like my Mickey slippers, Mama. I want to wear them to school."

"I know you like them, Sweetie," his mother said lovingly, thinking that she'd like to stay in hers, too.

Then she decided to paint Alec a picture of how he would face the day in his slippers. She did it by asking questions. "How do you think your slippers will work in the classroom?" she asked.

"Great!" the five-year-old said with enthusiasm.

"How do you think they'll work when you go outside for recess?" his mother asked.

"Oh!" little Alec said.

His mother was very quiet and didn't say another word, which gave Alec time to think.

"I gotta change into my tennis shoes, Mama. Can I pack my slippers in my backpack?"

"Sure, honey. Car leaves in four minutes."

❤ ❤ ❤

Alec's mother gave him a gift. She allowed him to think. With unconditional love and wise questions, she let him make a decision, knowing that he was smart enough to make a good one.

Which child got empathy instead of criticism? Which child is learning to think for him or herself? Which child is learning how it feels to succeed, to see him or herself as a thinking, able, and confident human being? Which, do you think, will have the higher self-concept?

How Parents Determine a Child's Self-Concept

FORMULA FOR LOW SELF-CONCEPT

Parents who:

- Find faults and criticize.
- Insist on doing everything for their children.
- Don't allow their children to experience the joy of independent success.

FORMULA FOR HIGH SELF-CONCEPT

Parents who:

- Offer empathy, understanding, and unconditional love.
- Allow their children to struggle and solve their own problems.
- Encourage children to learn to succeed through personal thinking and learning.

The Gift of Personal Success

A goal of Love and Logic is to make the home as similar as possible to the real world. Our children must know how to handle situations that appear without warning—that require them to think for themselves. When we give our children this gift, they begin to believe: "I've got what it takes!"

Take a look at Clive, a child who learned a lesson one day while he was at the airport. One person wanted to save him; another wanted to teach him to think. To save or not to save? That is the question.

Clive is at the airport for the first time in his life. What an exciting place! "Wow!" he thinks. "Look at all of this stuff!" The sights and sounds around him compel him to explore by venturing away from his mother. Suddenly, he stops dead in his tracks. "Where's Mom? I'm lost!" he realizes. Then the screaming begins. "I want my Mommy! I want my Mommy! I want my Mommy!"

A woman scoops him up in her arms and says, "Don't worry, we'll find your mom." She takes him to a nearby ticket agent and says, "This poor little boy is lost. We need to find his mommy. We need to help him!"

The ticket agent is a Love and Logic natural, and he's been watching Clive for some time. "What's your name?"

Clive softens his crying and whines, "Clive."

The observant ticket agent knows that Clive's mother is just around the corner, but he decides this may be a good time for an impromptu lesson. He smiles and asks, "What did your mother ask you to do, Clive?"

The boy says, "Sit in the chair she asked me to sit in, 'cause she went to the potty."

"Oh," says the agent. "And what did you do?"

The boy answers, "I got up and ran around."

"Bummer," says the agent. "What have you learned from this?"

The boy says, "I gotta stay where my mom sits me."

❤ ❤ ❤

The agent gave Clive a gift—the gift of wisdom. Every time we ask questions instead of merely rescuing the problem away from our kids, we give them tools that will last a lifetime. The agent saw the opportunity for Clive to learn something valuable.

The woman who had found the little boy was upset with the airline agent. She wanted to save the boy by immediately plopping him in his mother's lap. She looked at the agent and asked with disdain, "Why did you make that poor little boy think so hard and answer all of those questions before you showed him where his mother was?"

Responding with a soft smile, he simply answered, "So he knows he can."

Weighing learning experience against rescue, which is going to enhance a child's self-concept?

Every time we rescue our children, we erode their self-concept. Each time they solve a problem instead, we help them strengthen it.

The mother learned her lesson, too. It's not a wise decision to leave a small child unattended in an airport. The Love and Logic airline attendant asked her a lot of questions, too. But that's another story.

PRINCIPLE #2: *Share the Control*

Have you ever dropped coins into a soda machine—and nothing came out, including the coins? Have you ever misplaced your TV remote control? Have you ever waited in line at the grocery store when the clerk closes up just as it's finally your turn? Has your car ever failed to start when you were already late for an appointment?

Why are these situations so frustrating? They are irritating largely because the situation feels out of control. No matter how hard we kick the soda machine, no soda and no money come out. No matter how many times we turn the key, our car will not start. We feel powerless. It's that simple. Control is a basic human emotional need. It's something we crave so strongly that sometimes people will even hurt others—or themselves—to regain it. If you've ever seen a driver suddenly pull out from behind you, veer into another lane, and almost cause a head-on accident, you've seen the result of unmet control desires.

When children lack a sense of healthy control, some very sad things can happen.

Louisa's parents were very controlling with her while she was growing up. Her entire life was filled with rules. She was given no choices and always told how to dress, how to walk, what to say and how to say it.

"Don't do that!" her parents would say as she reached for colorful objects. "Don't cry!" they would say when she burst into tears. Her life was full of don'ts, and she never had opportunities to make decisions that concerned her welfare.

When she became a teenager, her parents simply said, "Don't do drugs, and don't have sex." There were no discussions, no questions about how Louisa felt about drugs or decisions about sex. When her parents found out, one day, that she was pregnant, they were shocked.

"We told her time and again not to have sex!" her father said. "The girl doesn't listen!" her mother added.

❤ ❤ ❤

Sadly, we at the Love and Logic Institute are not surprised. Louisa had found a way to show her parents that she was the one in control. Never having had that control, she lashed out in the only way she understood.

The Art and Science of Control

Battles over control benefit no one. They create tension and make warriors out of otherwise peaceful people. Love and Logic teaches parents the art of control. What is this "art"? Simply stated, give control away when you don't need it, so you can get some back when you do! Love and Logic also teaches the science of control. What is this "science"? Share control by giving the types of choices that *do not* cause a problem for you.

Sammy's father asked him, "Do you think it would be a good day to have fun at the park, or do you think it would be a good day to not have fun at the park?"

Sammy's eyes lit up, he got this funny look on his face, and he said, "Fun at the park, Silly!"

Dad is sharing control with some fun choices. Mom decides to join the fun.

"Okay. Now, let's see," she adds. "Do you want me to put your car seat on the left side of the backseat, or the right side?"

"I want to sit in the front!" says Sammy.

"Oh, that wasn't a choice. Let's put you on the right side." Not giving his child a chance to complain, Sammy's dad moves forward quickly. "Do you want me to drive the speed limit, or do you want me to drive a bit slower?"

"I want you to drive the speed limit, so we can get there fast!" Sammy says, partly exasperated by all these questions but, at the same time, feeling a great sense of control in telling his father how to drive the car.

When they get to the park, Sammy's mother asks, "Do you want to get on the swing first, or would you rather get on the slide?"

"I want to swing first!"

"Okay," says his dad. "Do you want me to push you, or do you want to swing by yourself?"

"Push me!" Sammy says, all excited.

"You want me to push you hard, or soft?"

"Hard!"

"Oh, okay," says his father. "Do you want to fall off and hurt yourself, or not fall off and hurt yourself?"

"Not!" says Sammy, perfectly seriously, although by now his mom and dad are laughing, so he does, too.

"Okay," says Sammy's mother. "You said you wanted to go on the slide. Do you want me to go on with you, or do you want me to stay here and watch?"

"You watch!" he says.

"You want me to catch you like a big monster and scare you when you come down, or do you want me to stand here and just be quiet?"

The wonderful thing about sharing this kind of control with young kids is that we can get silly with it and make it fun for ourselves as well as our kids. Sammy's mother notices that they have another fifteen minutes until they need to go. She signals her husband.

Sammy's dad says to his toddler, "Time to go, Sammy!"

Sammy is having so much fun, he doesn't want to go. He immediately whines, "I don't want to go!"

This is when a Love and Logic parent says, "Oops! I forgot to give you a choice! Would you like to leave now, or would you like to leave in fifteen minutes?"

Guess what this kid is going to choose.

"Fifteen minutes," the happy child says, claiming his control as if he's just won a prize. As this time expires, Dad says, "Okay! Fifteen minutes is over. Let's go.

Sammy immediately responds, "I don't want to go!"

Mom smiles and whispers, "Now, didn't we give you a lot of choices? This time, it's our turn for a choice. Thanks for understanding." With that information, Sammy looks at the dirt and whispers reluctantly, "Well—okay."

♥ ♥ ♥

Sammy's parents shared lots of control by providing plenty of choices. Did you notice that these choices were framed by firm limits? Did you notice how they were careful to give choices only on issues that did not create a problem for anyone on the planet? Did you notice how Sammy responded? These parents are making daily deposits into Sammy's wisdom account that are going to help Sammy—when he's a teenager and throughout his life.

Many parents set few limits when their kids are toddlers. They attempt to enforce them later when their children are adolescents. By that time, it's too late.

Love and Logic parents avoid the trap of waiting to set limits until their children are teens. Why? Because they understand that a child's ability to make choices, within the safety of limits, is the foundation of responsibility and wisdom—and they want to lay that foundation as early as possible. These parents also understand that even though children outwardly throw tantrums or complain about limits, inwardly they yearn for their parents to set and enforce them.

Sharing control within firm limits teaches wisdom and responsibility. Let's take a look at how one parent used a masterful combination of choices *and* limits to begin teaching responsibility.

Jim gazed lovingly at his little Cindy and asked, "Sweetie? Will you be picking up your toys today, or will I?"

When she forgot, he quietly picked them up and placed them on the top shelf of the hallway closet. Love and Logic parents know that children learn best from consequences when their parents avoid reminding or scolding. Jim kept his mouth shut and kept saying to himself, "Let the consequence do the teaching. Let the consequence do the teaching. Let the consequence do the teaching."

The next day, Cindy was a bit confused. "Where are my toys, Daddy?" she asked.

Jim responded softly, "How sad. Remember yesterday when I gave you a choice—to either pick them up or have me do it?"

"Yes, Daddy," she replied.

"Guess what happened!"

"You put them up?" she whined.

Jim simply nodded and whispered, "Yes. Will you be ready to try playing with them again tomorrow, or the day after?"

Cindy cried out, "Today! I want my toys today!"

Jim continued, "Today isn't a choice. Are you going to stop yelling, or do you need to have some 'being quiet' practice time in your room?"

Cindy stopped yelling and started to weep softly. Jim looked at her and asked, "Would you like a hug or no hug?"

Cindy looked up and said softly, "Hug."

The next day Cindy's toys reappeared for another Love and Logic training session. Cindy began playing with them but was quickly distracted by her favorite television show. Jim walked by and asked, "Cindy, will you be cleaning up your toys today, or will you be letting me?"

Cindy ran over and began tossing them into her toy chest. Jim couldn't resist asking, "Why are you picking them up instead of letting me?"

"Silly Daddy!" she responded. "I'm going to play with them tomorrow!"

❤ ❤ ❤

PRINCIPLE #3: *Provide a Strong Dose of Empathy Before Delivering Consequences*

There are many psychological theories about the role that discomfort plays in learning. Most suggest that human beings are programmed to avoid it. This makes sense. Most sane people will touch a hot stove only once before learning not to make a career out of it! As you may have learned from personal experience, when we hurt, we are often moved to make changes we might not otherwise make. Similarly, Love and Logic parents know that the pain of poor choices helps children learn to avoid mistakes. They also know that for this to happen, parents must allow it to happen in a loving way. Love and Logic parents are both strict and very loving at the same time.

Learning to See Consequences

Love and Logic parents love it when their children make mistakes. Why? Because the price tags of mistakes made by young children are much smaller than those made by teens. What's the price tag of wasting one's allowance at age five? It's insignificant. What's the price tag of wasting one's paycheck at age twenty-one? That's another story. What's the price tag of crashing one's tricycle? Perhaps a skinned knee. What's the price tag of crashing one's car at age sixteen? Perhaps one's life.

At the Love and Logic Institute, we believe that children pay very dearly when not allowed to make mistakes—and learn from them—when consequences are still small and "affordable."

> Robert's dad, Steve, had not gone fishing in a long time, and he was looking forward to this trip. This time Steve was taking his son, who was going fishing for the first time. They were both excited; however, by the time they made the hour-long drive, little Robert was what we call "three-quarters cranky"—not really a problem yet, but getting there.
>
> Robert started to whine. "I don't want to go fishing. This is boring. It's cold up here."
>
> "Well," said Steve, "let's give it a try since we came all this way." The two of them found a shallow part of the lake and walked out halfway, where it was only about a foot deep. There were some mossy rocks—fairly flat and not very high—jutting out of the water.
>
> When Steve looked up, he saw Robert starting to climb one of the low rocks. He thought to himself, "I better warn him and tell him to get off that rock. He's going to fall in. I know he is."
>
> What does a wise Love and Logic parent do at this point? The first question is always, "Will my child get hurt if he makes a mistake?" Steve quickly reviewed the situation. "It's

sandy here, not high, but he could get cold." The second question a parent asks is, "What will the child learn from this?" Steve thought, "He'll never do it again!"

A second later Steve heard a big splash. He turned and saw Robert jumping out of the water moving toward his father. "Daddy!" Robert cried, "You didn't tell me that rocks get slippery when they're wet!"

"Well," asked his father, with warmth and sadness in his voice, "what do you think?"

"I think they do!" little Robert said, as his dad pulled a towel from his backpack and wrapped it around his son.

"You're right!" said Steve. "You are one smart kid, you know that?"

❤ ❤ ❤

Do you think Steve contributed to Robert's self-concept by letting him make the slippery rock discovery on his own? Yes, because Robert could see himself learning something. Did Steve enjoy watching his son fall in? Not really, but he allowed it, because he knew it would be an opportunity for learning. The next time they went fishing, do you think little Robert watched the rocks closely to be sure of his footing? Absolutely. Robert is older now and loves to go fishing with his dad. From time to time, he even reminds his dad to be more careful!

How do Love and Logic parents look upon their young children's mistakes? With great joy! Rather than get angry or frustrated, they see mistakes as opportunities for their kids to think. They ask questions, wait for answers, and make heavy deposits into their children's wisdom accounts.

Unfortunately, some parents short-circuit or destroy the learning value of mistakes. How? By lecturing or responding with sternness or anger. Would Robert have learned so quickly about slippery rocks if Dad had responded with, "See! That's what you get! I hope you learned your lesson!"?

Why Anger Short-Circuits Learning

The "fight or flight" response exists in all human beings and is part of the "primitive" brain—that part of the brain governing basic survival instincts. When we feel threatened or in danger, our brain tells us, "This is unsafe! Get ready to fight, or get ready to run away!" When we deliver consequences with anger, children's brains go into "survival" mode rather than "learning" mode. They think more about escaping, or possibly getting revenge, than about how to make smarter choices in the future. In the survival mode, we cannot learn. Our focus is on getting away, fighting to be free, surviving.

Every time we use empathy, our kids' reasoning brains turn on. Every time we deliver threats or anger, their reasoning brains turn off. Empathy opens the mind to learning.

When parents provide empathy before delivering consequences, there is no "fight or flight" response. Caught in the flood of heartfelt understanding from a parent, a child is much less likely to become too angry or scared to learn. Under these circumstances, a child is also less likely to blame others for his or her mistake. Kids who are given empathy quickly develop a healthy voice inside of their heads. Instead of blaming or shifting responsibility, this voice asks, "How is my next decision going to affect my life? Which choice is going to be the wisest?" When our children face consequences, our spoonful of empathy is what makes the medicine of learning go down. Rather than set ourselves up as the enemy, wise parents use empathy in a way that makes the child's mistake the "bad guy," while keeping them, the parents, the "good guys."

Anger vs. Empathy

Consequences with Anger

Parent is stern or acts with anger:

"Stop spitting that food! Quit it! That's it! I'm sick and tired of this! You'll just have to go hungry!"

"For crying out loud! If you would just take care of your toys, they wouldn't break. No! I won't buy you another. What do you think? Do you think money grows on trees?"

"No, I am not taking you out for pizza. What do you expect after the way you behaved last time? I hope this teaches you a lesson!"

"Quit that whining! How many times do I have to tell you? Stop it! Go to your room!"

Consequence with Empathy

Parent says softly:

"How sad. Dinner is over."

"Bummer. I feel so sad when I break my things."

"This is so sad. We can have pizza sometime when I don't have to worry about tantrums at the restaurant."

"Uh-oh. So sad. Looks like a little bedroom time."

Remember:
Sincere empathy works wonders.
Sarcastic empathy backfires every time.

PRINCIPLE #4: *Share the Thinking*

Toni, a 14-year-old high school sophomore, was hanging out with some friends after school one afternoon before heading home. Another kid approached the group and whispered, "I just got some really wild stuff. You ain't gonna believe it! I was so wasted off it last time!"

"How much?" one of the kids mumbled.

"I'll make you a deal. You gotta try it! Listen! You guys can chip in, and each of you gets a little taste, eh?"

❤ ❤ ❤

Some school children encounter this kind of confrontation on a daily basis. What determines whether Toni will resist or fall prey to peer pressure? If all the other students decide to buy and use the drugs, will she do the same? How do we know? The factors that determine whether Toni will resist or succumb largely took place during the first five or six years of her life. Let's ask ourselves some questions.

• **How is Toni's self-concept?** How does Toni see herself? Does she believe that she's basically good and deserves a healthy life? Or does she feel poorly about herself—does she see life as hopeless and want to escape from it?

• **Does Toni have a healthy sense of personal control?** Has Toni been allowed to share control with her parents, or has she been prevented from having any? Is there any chance she might try drugs just to exert some independence or to show her parents who's really in control?

• **Does Toni have a strong relationship with her parents?** Does she enjoy pleasing them because she looks up to them? Or would nothing make her happier than to upset them?

• **Has she made plenty of mistakes and learned from them at an early age?** Has Toni already made lots of mistakes, experienced lots of empathy, and been held accountable? Does she have a healthy voice inside her head asking, "How is this next decision going to affect my life?"

• **Has Toni had lots of practice making choices, solving problems, and thinking for herself?** Has she had the opportunity to make decisions, think about her blunders, and consider their consequences? Or has someone else always told her what to do, solved her problems, and stolen any opportunity for her to practice thinking for herself?

Four Powerful Actions

There are four very powerful actions parents can take to raise kids who wind up making smart decisions about drugs, alcohol, sex, violence, and other serious matters. And the earlier, the better:

1. Raise a child who feels good about him- or herself.
2. Develop a strong bond of love and trust with your child.
3. Allow your child to make plenty of mistakes and learn from them at an early age.
4. Give your child plenty of practice thinking and solving problems.

All four of these powerful gifts allow children to develop stronger thinking skills.

How do we prepare our children for the tough, sometimes life-and-death decisions they'll have to make? The first step is showing that we care.

Every time we replace anger with empathy and caring, we help a child become better prepared to make wise decisions.

The more empathy and understanding we display, the more our children are forced to think about the pain they have created for themselves. The more anger or frustration we show, the less our children think—and the less they learn about solving problems.

Shared thinking means using lots of love and empathy and guiding a child toward solutions rather than either rescuing or automatically doling out punishment. Shared thinking starts when we ask questions.

"What a bummer, Ricky," his mother says to her five-year-old. "You gave your little sister a haircut, and now one side is really long, and the other is short and crooked. What are you going to do?"

Ricky scrunches up his shoulders and mumbles, "Don't know."

Mom responds softly, "Would you like to hear some ideas?"

"Uh-huh."

"One idea is to open your piggy bank and find enough money to have a barber fix her hair. How will that work?"

Ricky's eyes light up. "That sounds good, Mommy. How much will it cost?"

"I'm not sure. I'll show you how to dial the barber shop, and you can ask him how much he charges."

Ricky learns all about using the phone. His little finger pushes the buttons, he utters his question to the barber, listens, says good-bye, and hangs up. Tears are now running down his cheeks. Sniffling, he says, "The man said it's gonna cost six dollars. I only have three. What am I supposed to do?"

Mom replies with empathy. "This is so sad. I'm not sure." She pauses to add a little drama. "Want another idea?"

Ricky nods his head "yes."

"You can earn the other three dollars by helping me with a bunch of chores around here, like dusting and pulling up weeds in the yard. How would that work?"

Ricky looks up and says, "I hate chores."

Mom responds, "Another idea is to pay me with your Commander Bob Action Figure. How would that..."

With half-dollar-sized eyes, Ricky interrupts, "I'll do chores. I'll do chores!"

❤ ❤ ❤

Did you notice how much thinking Ricky had to do? Does Ricky get better prepared for the real world every time he has to make some decisions and choices that are difficult? And, does Ricky's mom have a lot more fun now that she's handling the problem with Love and Logic?

The principles of Love and Logic were developed when we were searching for common threads that might help us look at human behavior in a new way. Here's what we discovered.

**Successful people never fail,
because they turn their failures into wisdom.**

THE FOUR PRINCIPLES OF LOVE AND LOGIC

1. Build the Self-Concept. Everything kids learn and do affects how they see themselves, which, in turn, determines what they choose to do with their lives.

2. Share the Control. Control is like love. The more we give away, the more we get in return.

3. Offer Empathy, Then Consequences. Empathy allows children to learn from their mistakes instead of learning to resent adults.

4. Share the Thinking. Give your kids a life-long gift. Every time they cause a problem or make a mistake, allow them to think more about the solution than you do.

In other words, they keep learning, and they never give up. When we learned how well this applies to adults, we thought, how about kids?

We believe, from watching the young children in our own lives, as well as those we've met in our many years of work and travel, that it's never too early to start teaching wisdom. Wouldn't it be great if your children could learn, early on, that every choice they make affects the quality of their lives? A combination of love and logic can create this learning now, while they are still very young.

Love allows children to grow through their mistakes. Logic happens when we allow them to live with the consequences of their choices.

Love and Logic Experiment #1

Sharing the Control
Make a list of choices you can give your kids.

Make a list of the possible choices you can give your child. Here are some examples:

- "Would you like milk or juice with breakfast?"
- "Are you going to put your shirt on first or your pants on first?"
- "Are you going to wear your red shorts or your blue ones?"
- "Are you going to wear your coat or just carry it?"
- "Do you want a story before bed or no story?"
- "Do you want your night-light on or off?"
- "Are you going to brush your teeth now or in five minutes?"
- "Are you going to have carrots or peas for your vegetable?"

Remember to follow the Love and Logic guidelines for choices.

- Give 99% of choices when things are going smoothly.
- Provide choices only on issues that are not dangerous and don't create a problem for anyone else on the planet.
- Always offer two options, each a choice that makes you happy.
- In ten seconds flat, choose for the child if he or she doesn't.

See how many "deposits" you can make during the day.

See how many choices you can give during the day. Every choice you give becomes a "deposit" into your child's sense of healthy control. Have some fun. Even when choices seem small and a bit silly, they can be very powerful.

Make a "withdrawal" and see how your child reacts.

Pick an issue and choose not to give your child a choice. For example, "Please go to bed. Thank you."

If your child says something like, "I don't want to," try saying, "Don't I give you a lot of choices? This time it's my turn. Thank you." In Love and Logic language, we call this a "withdrawal."

See how your child reacts. Parents tell us over and over that the more choices, or "deposits," they make, the more cooperative their kids become.

CHAPTER TWO

It's Never too Early to Start

Better Now Than Later

Over the last twenty years, people have shared lots of fun Love and Logic success stories with us. Some have even used it successfully on their spouses! Kids can be a challenge, but with a few Love and Logic tools, you can up the odds that the early years—and beyond—will be a joy. What's the most important advice we give parents? Start as early in the child's life as possible.

Imagine that you've joined a camping trip for parents and their toddlers, and you're out in the wild, sharing this joyful experience with your four-year-old, who's been enjoying the new scenery, the crunchy, colored leaves, the tiny creatures he's discovered on the ground, and the sounds of the forest.

On the trip is a mother with a strong-willed toddler. Suddenly, the peacefulness of the forest is pierced by her child's whiny voice. "Mommy, look at this. Mommy, come over here and look at this worm. Mommy, hold my hand. Mommy, walk slower! Mommy, I want my pail and shovel so I can dig up this anthill! Mommy! Mommy! Mommy!"

The mother looks at you with some embarrassment and says, laughing nervously, "Jake is always so bossy. I don't know why."

You smile politely and move on, but you think to yourself, "I know why." This is a mother who is waiting until "later" to teach her child about responsibility and treating others with respect. You hope that she doesn't wait too much longer.

❤ ❤ ❤

Why do some parents wait until later to begin setting limits and enforcing them? Why do some allow their toddlers to get out of control and begin running the home? Some parents believe that young children are too young for discipline. Don't fall into this trap!

Three Common Myths about Discipline

Let's take a look at three common myths about discipline and young children.

MYTH #1: *Discipline and Learning Require Language*

Some people believe that children cannot learn or benefit from discipline until they can converse. Nothing is further from the truth! Can the family dog learn how to sit, stay, come, fetch, and lie down? I've never met a pooch who talked, but I have met some parents who seem to believe and act like the family dog is smarter than their kids. How sad!

By the age of nine months, human babies are more intelligent than any other creature on the planet. Wise parents begin teaching discipline during the early months through simple, loving actions—not words. If your child, for example, throws her bottle, remove it for a while. If your child won't sit in the high chair, fasten his seat belt. If your child runs away from you in the store, pick him up and gently carry him. Replace lectures, warnings, and lots of words with actions.

MYTH #2: *A Little Child Cannot Remember and Learn*

Have you ever promised a two-year-old a trip to the park or his favorite fast-food restaurant—and then forgotten to deliver? Will they ever let you forget? Never underestimate what young children can remember, and learn.

MYTH #3: *Setting Limits Will Break a Young Child's Spirit*

Some parents worry about making their toddlers angry. These parents seem to reason, "If I make sure that she's happy all the time, then she'll grow up to be a happy, nice person."

Wrong! At the Love and Logic Institute we're all for happy kids. That's why we encourage parents to set limits early. Why? Children who are made happy all of the time by their parents experience a major shock when they begin to grow up. Ironically, they soon become the most unhappy and demanding kids, and adults, you'll ever meet.

The First Weeks of Life

Would you be surprised to discover that the ability to learn basic cause and effect begins during a child's *first weeks* of life? Here are a few things a child learns right away:
- Screaming brings Mommy!
- I can move my foot!
- When I smile, Mommy smiles!

A child's ability to learn basic cause and effect begins during the first weeks of life

During the first weeks and months of life, infants quickly figure out whether their parents are going to set limits or become doormats. Remember Jake, the whiny kid on the camping trip? What did Jake's mother teach him early on? That she would be a doormat!

29

Love and Logic is all about being a good model for your kids by taking care of yourself in a loving way. Here's how Billy's mother accomplished this.

I (Charles) was walking behind Billy and his mother at the zoo one day. They were having a great time. All of a sudden, Billy began to whine. His mother ignored him.

"Mommy!" Billy said. "Why aren't you listening?"

His mother kept walking and asked softly, "Why do you think?"

"But why?" Bill insisted.

His mother kept walking, smiled, and asked again, "Honey, why do you think?"

Billy became silent for a few seconds, then sweetened the tone of his voice and said, "Because you listen to me when I use big boy words?"

"Oh, yes, Honey!" she said warmly, "You figured that out all by yourself!" She stopped walking, reached down, and gave him a hug. They continued to have a great time!

❤ ❤ ❤

Which kid would you rather be around? Jake or Billy? Which child do you think will lead a happier life in the long run?

> **When people ask, "When can we start using
> Love and Logic with our children?" we say,
> "Start when they're babies." Sometimes we even add,
> "Start when they're cute, so they will stay that way!"**

Bonding Builds Trust and Responsibility

When our children are infants, our primary goal must be to develop a strong, caring bond. Why is this bond so essential? In the following chapter, we'll learn that bonding builds a foundation of trust that lasts a lifetime. Furthermore, this foundation of trust influences every relationship a person ever experiences!

Children without this foundation tend to experience chronic relationship problems, severe anger, and often become destructive to themselves and others.

How is this foundation constructed? Every time our infant cries, and we respond by meeting his or her needs, we lay in place another building block of trust. On a deep emotional level, the child reasons, "The world is a good place—and I'm good!"

Bonding Requires Limit-Setting

In the next chapter, we'll also learn that bonding requires basic limit-setting. When children fail to find loving limits, they feel scared. How do they tell us? By acting out!

When children act out, what they're really saying is, "Please love me enough to set some limits!"

Little ten-month-old Linda was beginning to resist the strained carrots her mother, Selena, was offering her for lunch. At first, Linda had seemed to enjoy the carrots. Then, little by little, she became crankier and crankier. Suddenly she became so cranky that she spit them out—all over the tray, her high chair, her bib—and her mommy.

Selena immediately put down Linda's tiny spoon and said, with gentle, sweet sorrow in her voice, "How sad. Lunch is over." She quickly but gently raised the tray of her daughter's high chair, lifted Linda out of her seat, and took her to her crib. She said nothing more.

❤ ❤ ❤

Did you notice how Mom used Love and Logic to lock in the empathy? Did you notice how Mom used simple, loving actions instead of anger, lectures, or threats? This child may be very young, but she's already learning about limits, consequences, and how much her mommy loves her.

The "Terrible Twos" Can Be Terrific

We often hear people argue that two-year-olds are too young to benefit from Love and Logic, because they can't understand or remember. At the Love and Logic Institute, we don't agree, and here's why. Have you ever promised a two-year-old a lollipop and failed to deliver? Have you ever told your toddler you would take him to his favorite ice cream shop and then forgotten to make the trip? If so, you'll have to acknowledge what we've learned at Love and Logic: By age two, long-term memory is firmly locked in!

Meet Curtis. Like many kids his age, Curtis's favorite word is "No." He loves the sound of the word and says it many times in the course of a day. While his mother used to interpret this as Curtis's way of being disagreeable and ornery, she's learned that it's really a natural behavior for a two-year-old. Best of all, she now has some skills for handling it.

> The primary developmental task of a toddler is to establish autonomy, and Curtis loves to practice being autonomous! "No!" he says when his mother asks him to hold her hand. "No!" he shouts when she asks him to wait for her. "No!" he yells when she tells him not to leave an aisle without her.
>
> When they went shopping, Curtis loved to run away from his mother in the store. As much as his mother understood his desire for independence, his brief disappearances would make her nervous. She decided to take some action.
>
> Unbeknown to Curtis, she had a friend follow her to the store and wait in the parking lot. As Mom began her shopping, Curtis wandered. This was a dream come true for Curtis's mom. He was misbehaving, and this was her opportunity to give Curtis a gift of wisdom.
>
> As she caught up with him, she dialed her cell phone. Into the receiver, she said, "Okay. It's time. Come and get him."
>
> Curtis's eyes grew to the size of coffee can lids as Mom's friend led him out of the store. He was even unhappier when he had to use his Zooming Wheels Racer to pay for the baby-sitting. What a bummer!

The following week, Curtis's mom was getting ready to go shopping. She said to Curtis, "I have to go shopping, Sweetie. Do you want to come with me?"

"Yes!" announced Curtis, using a word he rarely uses.

"What's the rule when we go shopping, Honey?"

"I stay with Mommy!" Curtis responded, without missing a beat.

"That's right," his mother said. "Way to go!"

When they reached the store, Curtis was so excited that he experienced temporary memory impairment. What did Mom do? With a lilt in her voice, she sang, "Uh-oh!"

Curtis quickly looked up at his mother, smiled, and ran to her side. From that day on, shopping became a pleasure instead of a pain—for both of them.

❤ ❤ ❤

Curtis's mommy conducted a little Love and Logic training session. Did you notice how she replaced anger with empathy? Did you notice how Curtis got a chance to learn about limits, consequences, and cause and effect? Did Curtis have to do some thinking on his own, or did his mother rescue him? Do you suppose Curtis sees his mom as very strong *and* very loving at the same time?

When It's Time for Potty Training

There are many wonderful ways to help our kids think for themselves and help them become wiser. The following is a story about Harry, who learned, along with his family, that potty training can be fun, for both parent and child.

Little Harry lives in a house that has two bathrooms—one upstairs and one downstairs. One morning, his father said, "Hey, Harry! You want to use the upstairs potty or the downstairs potty?"

"Upstairs! Upstairs potty!" Harry said.

A Love and Logic parent, his father smiled and said, "You want to have fun while we're doing this, or not have fun?"

The great thing about choices with little kids is that they love making them—even when the options we give seem a bit silly to us. The decisions they make on their own make them feel important, leave them with a sense of control, and give them lots of chances to exercise their brains.

Harry looked at his dad as if he were crazy and giggled, "Fun! I want to have fun!"

"Great," said his dad. "Do you want to bring a drink in with you, or do you want to wait until you're done?"

"Wait till I'm done!"

"Do you want to bring Clarence, your stuffed sea otter, with us, or do you want to leave him?"

"Bring him!" Harry says, as he goes to retrieve his favorite stuffed playmate.

Now, Harry's dad moves to the next step—modeling. Although some parents might find it a little embarrassing, modeling is the best way to teach your kids just about anything. Harry's dad thinks it's great.

"Hey! I really have to use the bathroom!" he says enthusiastically to his son. "Why don't you come in with me? Let's go. Let me show you how it's done!"

He shows his son how he uses the bathroom. "This is so much fun!" he laughs. "Someday when you're big enough, I bet you'll be able to use the potty like me! Then you can have fun, too! Boy! I love using the potty! I can even wipe myself! Check this out!" He flushes the toilet and waves, "Bye-bye!" as they look into the toilet.

❤ ❤ ❤

The logic here is clear. Kids want to be like their parents. Whatever parents do, kids naturally want to be able to do, too. And if parents think it's fun, kids will, too. So, parents have some choices when it comes to potty training:

- We can allow ourselves to become embarrassed and refuse to model this skill.
- We can fight with our kids over the issue and try to force them to be ready before they actually are.
- We can decide to have some fun, take the pain out of the process, and build strong relationships with our kids. How? Use lots of choices—and model, model, model!

When parents offer choices, model, and make a task fun, learning happens quickly.

When Accidents Happen

If you know how to ride a bike, you probably remember falling a few times before finding the right balance. When we're learning something new, accidents are bound to happen. So it is with our children when they are at potty-training age.

Successful parents dole out empathy and say, "Oh, you had an accident! That's too bad! I love you, Sweetie." They take their time and don't rush anything, because there's no set timetable for potty training. Every child has his or her own unique schedule of development.

Some children potty train at two, some when they're four, and some at every age in between. It all depends on the child. A wise parent locks in the empathy and waits for kids to develop the skill on their own. Then, when a child is successful, a parent can say, "You did it! I bet that feels great!"

Unsuccessful parents have a pattern, too. When their kids make a mistake, they get upset, or angry. They say, "You messed your pants again! That's not nice! We don't do that! Now you better learn how to do this right! You're going to sit here until you use the potty!"

You can guess what happens. The child sees frustrated parents, and the child gets frustrated, too. Like any task we're expected to perform under pressure, potty training becomes an undesirable chore. What a bummer!

Three Years and Beyond: Too Much Fun?

A parent, who'd been using Love and Logic with his three-year-old son, once asked, "Is it okay to be having this much fun? I've heard my friends complain about their kids and, frankly, I'm having a great time with mine. Am I doing something wrong?"

One of the beauties of Love and Logic is that it can make parenting fun again. When children reach the age of three, parents get to be even more creative. What makes this age so exciting? Kids are now able to do a lot more of their own thinking—and learning!

Oscar, the parent who had owned up to having so much fun, told us about his friend's child. Every morning, the mother has a fifteen-minute battle with her child over whether or not he is going to wear his coat. Oscar was bewildered. He kept remarking, "Why is the coat issue such a big deal? I never fight with my kid over that!"

To understand the difference between this child and Oscar's child Natalie, we asked Oscar what he does. Here's his story.

> Oscar said to his five-year-old daughter, Natalie, "Time to head for school. It's chilly out. Do you want to wear your coat, or do you want to carry it and see how long you can do without it?"
>
> As soon as we heard Oscar's question, we immediately understood why he has no problem with Natalie. He gives her a choice, but both options mean that she has to take her coat with her.
>
> "I'll take it," Natalie said, "and see how long I can do without it."
>
> As they drove to school, Natalie sat in the backseat and said, "I'm cold, Daddy. Turn up the heat." Natalie's coat was on the seat next to her.
>
> Oscar described what he felt like saying, "Well, put your coat on, dummy!" Instead, he remembered his Love and Logic training and opted to say something a bit more loving and effective. "What do you think you can do?" he asked his daughter. Then he shut his mouth and waited a few seconds.

"Oh!" said Natalie, stopping to think and then declaring, "I better put my coat on."

❤ ❤ ❤

What did Natalie's father feel like saying in that moment? Probably something a bit sarcastic! But he didn't. Instead, he said, "Good thinking! You figured that out by yourself! You're such a smart little girl—got brains like your daddy!"

Did you notice how her father held back the impulse to tell her what to do—or to put her down? Did you see how he did not rescue her, but allowed her to learn from her choice? Who was doing the thinking? Did you notice how her father's questions caused her to think and reach a decision on her own?

At the age of three and beyond, when kids are able to do more thinking for themselves, parents have many more opportunities to help build their children's self-concept. Asking questions and allowing children to make decisions gives them skills they will use throughout their lives. It's never too early to start!

Children who can solve their own problems wind up feeling better about themselves.

So many kids! So little time! But because we're sure that these examples are helpful to parents, we want to offer you as many as we can. Over and over again, parents tell us how helpful these stories are to them. Here's a fun one about Jonathan, who, unwittingly, grew a lot wiser one night after visiting with a friend.

Jonathan was invited to spend the night with a little friend of his, a neighbor who lived a block down the street. He had a great time. The next day, as he trudged through the grocery store with his mother, she asked, "Why are you so tired?"

"Because Timmy and I were up all night watching movies!" Jonathan moaned.

Jonathan's parents were angry with the parents of his little friend. The nerve, they thought, allowing little children to stay awake all night! Then, they remembered: Wise parents hope and pray for mistakes when the price tags are small. They waited for Jonathan to be invited back.

A couple of weeks later, Jonathan was invited to another sleepover. His parents, who had made a plan, put it to work. Before driving Jonathan to his friend's home, his father said, "Hey! You gonna stay up all night again? I think you should. Stay up all night, Sweetie! Then when you come home, you can tell us all about it!"

"Yeah!" Jonathan said, all excited. "Great! We can stay up all night and watch a fun movie!" he said.

The next day, Jonathan came home, and his parents couldn't wait to ask, "What happened? Did you have fun? Did you stay up and make it through the night?"

Jonathan quickly answered, "I didn't want to."

Biting their tongues, his parents asked, "Why not?"

"Well," Jonathan said, "the last time I did that I was soooo tired!"

❤ ❤ ❤

Instead of being angry, Jonathan's parents realized that their neighbors had done them a big favor. They had, unknowingly, instigated a mistake that had a small price tag and allowed their child to learn an important lesson on his own.

All You Need to Know

Each child is born with an individual temperament and time clock of development. Children learn new skills when they are ready. Toddlers go after independence with the determination of Alexander Hamilton. Preschoolers create their own worlds with the imagination of Walt Disney. We don't have to be experts in child development to use Love and Logic. We also don't need a degree in child psychology to be a great parent. All we really need to know is that kids are ready for Love and Logic as soon as they're old enough to spit food across the table or crawl away when we're trying to change their diapers.

Love and Logic Experiment #2

Putting an End to Whining

Teach your child the difference between a whiney voice and a "big" one.

The next time your child whines, try saying, "I hear you when your voice sounds big instead of whiney."

Next, have some fun with your child and model the difference between whiney and not whiney.

"Sweetie, a whiney voice sounds like this, 'I waaaant it. Give it to meeee!' A big voice sounds like, "Mommy, may I please have this?' I hear big voices not whiney voices.

When your child begins to whine, go hard of hearing.

When your child begins to whine, pretend you can't hear it. Or say something like, "There's this strange little squeak in my ear. I can't tell what it is. Must be a little buggie or something."

If your child continues to whine, become a broken record.

If your child continues to whine, smile and keep asking, "Why can't I hear you?" Parents are always amazed how fast their kids learn to talk "big."

For an example, review the story of Billy on page 30.

CHAPTER THREE

Planting the Seeds of Responsibility, Kindness, and Empathy

Basic Needs in the Early Years

Have you ever met a child who just didn't seem to care about others? Have you ever met a child who seemed to be missing something down deep in his soul? More and more children are growing up without the basic seeds of responsibility and kindness, and their common missing element is love and empathy for others and themselves. Some of these kids appear troubled, yet quiet and secretive. Others seem ready to explode at any moment. Still others, at first glance, appear perfectly charming, yet prove themselves manipulative and hurtful.

Warning signs in such children become evident early in their lives as we watch them interact with other people. Let's take a look at Joshua as he plays in the backyard.

Six-year-old Joshua is digging dirt in the yard while his mother plants some flowers. When the telephone rings, his mom goes indoors. As soon as she's out of sight, Josh picks up a rock and throws it through the window of their garage. He's been thinking about doing this for an hour, but his mother's been watching him.

Josh smiles when he hears the crash. Then he dusts off his hands on his pants and goes back to digging. As his mother runs out of the house, she asks him what happened.

"Tommy, from next door. He threw a rock and broke it," Josh responds with practiced sincerity.

Angry, Joshua's mom rushes back into the house to call Tom's mother. When she returns to the yard, she's even angrier. "Tommy's mother tells me he isn't home, Josh, and hasn't been home all day."

Joshua responds, "Well, she's lying! I don't know who threw it! If you loved me, you would believe me!" Quietly, he looks down and begins playing again as if nothing has transpired.

Frustrated beyond belief, Mom lectures, "I think you do! Tommy's mother was standing by her dining room window when she saw *you* throw the rock!"

Joshua looks back and proclaims, "She's lying! I hate her!"

"Did you do it?" Mom asks again. "Why did you do it?" she begs. No answer. Past her limit, she picks him up, takes him in the house, and places him in a chair. Immediately, he bursts into angry tears and begins to scream, "I hate her! I hate her!"

Later in the day, unknown to anyone, Joshua kicks his dog. As it yelps and runs away, Joshua feels a little better.

❤ ❤ ❤

Sadly, there are many Joshuas in the world. His actions are upsetting, because he did what he did on purpose! Afterward, he felt no remorse. When confronted by his mother, he blamed his actions on another child. He even accused an adult of lying! When he was alone again, he took out his rage on the dog.

The long-term consequences for children like Joshua are always sad and often tragic. They have difficulty maintaining relationships and lead unsatisfying lives. Those they know become the brunt of ongoing hurt. As they grow up, they often experience a multitude of problems—multiple divorces, illegitimate children, frequent job losses, substance abuse, and so on. And, many wind up with alcohol and drug problems. In extreme cases, these are the children who go to school and shoot their classmates.

The good news is that there is hope for children like Joshua, but only if their parents seek competent professional help as early in the child's life as possible. Here's some even better news. There are proven, practical ways of *preventing* problems like this from ever happening in the first place—ways of raising responsible, caring kids. Ricki, below, is a good example of this type of child.

Ricki walks through a neighborhood park with her father. They like to play baseball together, and she's learning to be a pitcher. While her dad stops to say hello to a friend, Ricki discovers a collection of rocks near some trees. She picks one up and pitches it as far as she can, to see how far she can throw. Proud of the distance she threw the first one, she picks up another and flings away.

As her father continues to visit with his friend, Ricki lets go of still another. Everyone nearby turns to see where the crashing sound came from, and nobody looks at Ricki. To her utter amazement, not to mention terror, she realizes that her arm is stronger than she thought. The Park Center building now has a broken window.

Embarrassed by her actions, Ricki observes that no one seems to know that she threw the rock. Too stunned to speak, she says nothing. Her father notices that she's a little quiet on the way home and obviously has something on her mind, but he chalks it up to her being lost in a little girl daydream. He thinks to himself, "Sure glad my kid didn't break that window!"

That night Ricki lies in bed unable to fall asleep because of the guilt she feels. She gets out of bed at two in the morning to wake her father. She stands in his bedroom doorway with tears running down her face.

"Daddy?" she sobs. "I was the one who did it. I broke the window!"

What a difference, compared to Joshua! Ricki did not intend to break the window. Instead, she was in one of those experimental modes that kids sometimes get into—wanting to see what happens when you put ketchup in your orange juice, put your feet into your sweatshirt sleeves, or throw a rock as far as you can. Unlike Joshua, who longed to break the window and moved ahead in a devious way, Ricki's action was based on an impulsive thought. She acted on it and was surprised—by her own action as well as by the broken window. Further, Ricki's heart wouldn't allow her to continue deceiving her dad. Unlike Joshua, she felt true remorse.

After Ricki and her father reported the accident to the Park Center and Ricki agreed to pay her dad back for the window by doing some chores around the house, her father said, "That was quite a throw, Sweetie. Thanks for telling me." Giving her a tight hug, he whispered, "I love you."

Kids like Ricki don't have a war zone rumbling inside them. They experience angry moments like the rest of us, but most of the time they're happy, healthy kids. Furthermore, they're terrible liars. Those who try to lie about what they've done have a tone in their voice, a look in their eye, that gives them away. They lose sleep and appetite over misbehavior and, deep down, feel really sad about hurting other people or property—even if they don't get caught.

What Makes the Difference between Joshua and Ricki?

What's the difference between a child who cannot sleep at night because of personal misbehavior and a child who premeditates destructive actions, doesn't seem to care, blames other people, and apparently suffers no genuine remorse?

A child's ability to love and respect oneself and others is primarily determined by how well that child's basic needs were met during the first two years of life.

We cannot overemphasize the importance of the first years of life. Even more helpful than simply accepting its truth is seeing what makes it true. The best way to understand what happens during this time is to, metaphorically speaking, "stand in an infant's shoes"—get inside that child's skin, and lie in that child's crib.

Learning to Trust

Imagine that you're an infant, growing up in a healthy family. You're lying in your crib, looking up at the ceiling. From your point of view, life's pretty good.

All of a sudden, you don't feel so good. Life really starts to stink. You've just messed your diaper! You cry out, "Waa! Waa! Waa....!" Very soon, somebody comes to look at you. That person picks you up, smiles at you, notices that your diaper is full and changes it. Deep in your soul, you feel, "Life is good!"

A few minutes later, you're lying in your crib again, and everything is fine. Minutes later, you get a strange feeling. You feel empty. You're hungry. You cry out. Again, someone comes to look at you. That person picks you up again, smiles at you, figures out that you might want some food, and feeds you. Now, you're feeling okay. Life is good again!

Every time an infant's basic needs are met, a seed of trust and kindness is planted in that child's mind and heart. On a deep emotional level, a child feels, "Since people are taking such good care of me, I must be really good—and so are they!" In the 1970s, our friend and colleague Dr. Foster Cline described this process in what he termed "The Trust Cycle."

THE TRUST CYCLE STEP #1: The Child Has a Basic Need

At the beginning of the cycle, the child has a need—he or she may be hungry, cold, lonely, bored, have a messy diaper, or experience some other type of pain or discomfort. These are *basic* needs—the ones that MUST be addressed for the child's survival. On an instinctual level, a child knows that he or she will die if these needs are not met. What would you do if you knew you were going to die, but you couldn't walk or speak? Probably what any human being would do—scream and cry with all of the rage you can muster.

The Trust Cycle

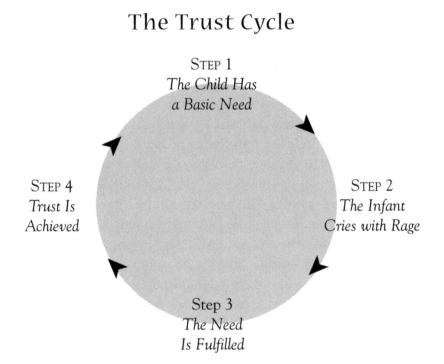

STEP 1
*The Child Has
a Basic Need*

STEP 4
*Trust Is
Achieved*

STEP 2
*The Infant
Cries with Rage*

Step 3
*The Need
Is Fulfilled*

THE TRUST CYCLE STEP #2: The Infant Cries with Rage

As the infant lying in the crib, you begin to scream, kick, and cry. "I'm going to die if somebody doesn't come and take care of me," you realize on a deep instinctual level. "This is a life and death matter!"

THE TRUST CYCLE STEP #3: The Need Is Fulfilled

Suddenly, somebody comes along, smiles at you, sniffs you, picks you up, finds out what's wrong, and finally feeds you or meets some other need. As this happens, you receive the basic components of human bonding—eye contact, smiles, touch, and relief from pain or discomfort.

Basic Emotional Components of Bonding

- Eye contact
- Smiles
- Hugs, holding, and touch
- Relief from pain and discomfort

Just as food is essential to keep your baby alive, so are all the nutrients of bonding. We have learned that an infant who gets no eye contact, no smiles, and no hugging or holding will die. "Failure to thrive" is the term for this tragic condition.

An infant will die without food, but also may die without eye contact, smiles, and touch.

The first time you make eye contact with your child and each of you explores the magical appearance of the other, one of your child's unspoken needs is satisfied. Just as a picture is worth a thousand words, so is a look. By looking into your baby's eyes and allowing your child to look into yours, wordless communication takes place.

A smile speaks volumes about how you feel about your child. From the very beginning, your baby recognizes you and smiles to acknowledge attachment to you. The child who *sees* smiles learns *how* to smile, and every time you share one, the bond grows. The child develops a smile in his or her heart.

From the moment of birth, the sound of your heartbeat, your physical contact, and your warmth give your child a sense of security and trust. When this is missing early in life, children harden. Their hearts close to themselves and others, and they begin to believe that the only way to survive is to hurt others.

THE TRUST CYCLE STEP #4: Trust Is Achieved

As you are being fed, cleaned, held, etc. You feel, "Oh, what a relief! This person just saved my life! This is a good world I live in! People can be trusted to take care of me. I must really be loved!" A child who has a need, cries out and gets the need fulfilled, begins to develop a sense of security and trust in the world.

Infants who know that their basic needs are going to be met develop love and kindness in their hearts. Those who don't, spend their lives angry at the world and themselves.

As each cycle ends and a child's need is realized, a notch of trust is etched into their being. The Trust Cycle goes 'round and 'round many times in the course of a day, a week, a year. Every time it's completed, the child develops a stronger level of trust—not only in the caregiver, but also in society. Simply stated, an infant's first human relationship strongly shapes how he or she views the world. When we have a basic feeling of trust toward society, we tend to live by its laws, morals, and ethics. When we lack this trust, we do whatever we can to undermine core values—we lie, steal, cheat, hurt, and even kill.

Broken Trust

In more and more families today, there are significant breaks taking place in The Trust Cycle. The reasons, many and varied, are sometimes within a parent's control and sometimes not:

1. Abuse and neglect.
2. The child's parent(s) have problems with alcohol or drugs, have a severe mental illness or some other serious problem.
3. The child's parents are injured, killed, or become very ill—in war, or a personal disaster.
4. The child has an illness that a parent wants to cure, but can't.
5. The child has been adopted or placed in foster care after failing to be cared for properly.
6. The child has spent most of his or her first months of life in poor quality day care.

Noncaring or sick parents aren't the only ones who may have kids with these problems. Some families have children who were born with an illness. In these cases, loving parents want to take away the child's pain, but can't figure out what's wrong. By the time a child gets to the doctor, perhaps months later, the child has felt, over and over again, that the world is a painful place.

Breaks in the Trust Cycle

The Child Fills with
Rage and Hatred
Toward the World

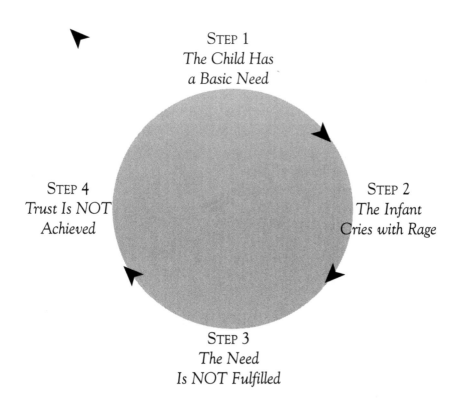

STEP 1
The Child Has
a Basic Need

STEP 4
Trust Is NOT
Achieved

STEP 2
The Infant
Cries with Rage

STEP 3
The Need
Is NOT Fulfilled

Consequences of Breaks in the Cycle

The major consequence of a chronic, ongoing break in the trust cycle is "down-to-the-marrow-of-the-bones" rage. This child is angry at the world—feels betrayed. "What kind of world is this? Nobody is going to take care of me! I hate this place!"

**A child who reaches this point
makes an unconscious decision. "From now on,
I'm going to hurt people before they hurt me!"**

Some Consequences of Significant Breaks in The Trust Cycle
- Excessive anger and rage
- Destructiveness
- Chronic lying
- Lack of remorse
- Poor problem-solving skills
- Cruelty to animals
- Lots of pain for everyone

The consequences of chronic breaks in The Trust Cycle during a child's first year of life can take a heavy toll on parents, as well as on the child. Kids who are filled with rage have trouble functioning in the healthy ways that most of us take for granted. Since they don't see themselves in a positive light, they cannot see the rest of the world that way either. Life is painful for these kids, and for everyone around them.

Most of us are caring people who tend to our children's needs and respond to them with consistency. Occasionally, we can't or don't figure out our kids' needs, and we sometimes miss. An occasional miss is not going to scar our kids for life. Nobody is perfect! Serious problems can develop when basic needs are unmet on a *chronic* and *ongoing* basis.

All we really need to understand is that wise parents do whatever they can to meet their young children's needs. They smile, they hold, they rock, they gaze into the child's eyes, and they prove to the child that people can be trusted. If the child continues to cry and cannot be soothed, wise parents consult with a qualified medical professional.

The Difference between Needs and Wants

Over the years, there have been some books in the marketplace suggesting that parents should let their infants "cry it out." Those of us who value what Love and Logic has to teach believe that parents who allow their infants to "cry it out"—who do not respond to their babies' basic needs—create serious breaks in the trust cycle. Some of these books may be confusing kids' needs with kids' wants. Let's take a look at the difference.

It seems obvious that when children become adults, they still have a need for food, water, and shelter. Less obvious is that we all continue to need love, a sense of belonging, feelings of self-competence, and a healthy realization of control. These are BASIC NEEDS, and, as we grow, they remain fairly constant.

As infants become toddlers, they also develop a wide array of desires. As Foster Cline says, "A two-year-old is not only a bundle of needs, but now is a bundle of wants."

**We all have difficulty, from time to time,
telling the difference between our needs and our wants.**

As adults we may think we "need" a brand new sports car or home entertainment system. We may believe we "need" to win a million dollars. A kid may declare a "need" for a battery-operated truck, the newest doll, or a new video game that "everyone else has." In truth, we—and our kids—don't need these things. We *want* them. People who can't tell the difference tend to lead painful lives. They have money and relationship problems, and they're chronically unhappy.

In today's world, has this become a societal epidemic? Some people lie and cheat in order to acquire something they want. Others rob, steal, and even kill because they don't get what they want. Countries go to war over wanted power and pieces of land—things they believe they *need*. At one time or another, we're all guilty of allowing wants to live in our hearts as needs.

**Do your children a favor.
Teach them the difference between wants and needs.**

Meeting Needs and Limiting Wants

When it comes to toddlers and preschoolers, our responsibility as parents is to accomplish three tasks:

- **Consistently meet basic needs.** We complete The Trust Cycle and provide our children with the essentials they need for a kind, loving heart.
- **Distinguish between kids' needs and wants.** We show our kids that there's a difference between what they need and what they want.
- **Set limits.** Continue to meet basic needs while setting limits on our child's "wants."

As the second year of life approaches, the role we play as parents must adapt. To maintain the parent-child bond, we must also begin setting limits on wants. Does every child yearn down deep for the love and security of firm limits? Absolutely!

Unfortunately, many parents believe that if they give their children free rein—allow them to do anything they want—their kids will be happy and will grow into responsible, loving adults. Nothing could be further from the truth!

As we now know, to become kind and responsible people, kids must develop a healthy bond with the adults who care for them. What is often forgotten is that this bond can only be maintained when loving limits are regularly set and faithfully enforced. Why? Limits say to your child:

- "I love you enough to keep you safe."
- "I love you enough to help you feel secure."
- "I care enough to teach you the difference between your needs and wants."
- "I care enough to prepare you for the real world."

Healthy bonding requires both love and limits

If you've ever seen a child a parent might call "bossy"—like Jake who kept his mother hopping on their camping trip—you've seen the result of setting no limits at a young age. Although Jake may appear to be in control of his mother, down deep he is feeling totally out of control. His little subconscious mind is probably wondering, "If Mommy can't control me, who will keep me safe? Why doesn't she love me enough to set some limits?"

The Irony of Setting No Limits

Isn't it ironic that kids whose parents fail to set and enforce limits feel unloved and angry? Although they tend to test and protest, we have learned over and over again that limits are what kids really want. Invariably, when we talk with out-of-control teenagers or adults who were juvenile delinquents and lucky enough to survive, we ask them, "If you could go back to when you were a child, what would you change?" Most of them say something like, "I wish my parents had reeled me in when I was a kid. Why didn't they make me behave?"

A counselor we know sat down with a teenager who'd led a pretty rough life. She had been promiscuous, had become pregnant, and was in trouble with the law. She went on to describe how she had smoked pot and guzzled beer with her dad as a ten-year-old. When the counselor asked her what she thought about it, her eyes lit up with rage and she said, "I hate him!" Surprised, the counselor said, "You had so much freedom. Why do you hate your father?"

Even more surprised, the teen responded, "I hate him 'cause he let me do anything I wanted. He never made me behave. Look at me now!"

External Controls Inspire Creativity

Most parents accept that we don't help our toddlers and preschoolers when we give them too much freedom. Still, they remain concerned about putting a lid on children's personality or individuality. If we lead with too strong a hand—set too many limits—will we put a damper on some creative aspect of our child, burying it forever? Will we frighten our kids away from being free to express who they really are?

At Love and Logic conferences we have told thousands of parents:

**If you want your children to have internal controls
and inner freedom, you must first
provide them with external controls.**

A child who is given boundaries, and choices within those boundaries, is actually freer to be creative, inventive, active, and insightful. How you expose your kids to the life around them— how you encourage them to use their creativity *within* limits, by using yours—is key to developing their personal identity and freedom. Setting limits does not discourage inventiveness.

**The world is full of limits within which we all must live.
Give your children a gift. Teach them how to
be creative within these limits.**

Love and Logic Experiment #3

Strengthening the Bond

Pay attention to what your child loves and write these things down.

Over the course of a week, pay close attention to what your child really loves the very most. Here are some typical examples:

- A certain stuffed animal or toy
- Drawing or coloring
- Playing a certain fantasy game, such as "princess" or "super hero" etc.
- A certain shirt, pair of shoes, or pair of pants
- A silly word or saying
- A specific type of food
- Playing catch

At least three times a week, walk over to your child, smile, and notice these interests.

On one day, you may say something like, "I noticed you like to draw." Two days later you may say, "I noticed you really love those sneakers." A day or two later you might say, "I noticed you like to play good guys and bad guys."

DO NOT end these statements with something like, "That's great!"

Why do we say this? Over the past twenty years, we have found that kids almost always respond best if we can avoid adding any type of judgment to our noticing. Why? Many children seem to reason, "If she thinks this is great, maybe she will think the next thing I do is not great."

Our primary goal here is to show that we notice our children's interests rather than judging these interests as either good or bad.

Notice how your child reacts.

Most parents are really amazed how well this little "noticing" routine works! They often say things like, "My daughter just beams with joy when I do this." They also comment that their children are typically more compliant when they've been using this tool. Why is this so? When children feel that their parents notice and value their interests, they are always happier and more cooperative.

CHAPTER FOUR

Love Them Enough to Take Care of Yourself

Parenting Doesn't Have to Be Brain Surgery

Parents often feel overwhelmed because they've been led to believe that they have to be experts in child development in order to raise responsible, healthy kids. Hogwash! In our Love and Logic approach, we ask parents not to over-complicate their lives with complex theories or techniques. What is our advice to you? Keep it simple and have some fun.

Effective parenting is achieved when parents learn a few simple tools so well that they can pull them off with a smile on their face and no sweat on their brow.

Over the past twenty-five years, we've realized that the four basic principles you learned in Chapter 1 apply to all ages, from little babies to adults. Rather than rethink parenting for each age, the goal of this book is to give you specific examples of how to apply a single philosophy to all young children. The goal of this book is to make your life easier—not harder.

The Two Rules of Love and Logic

Love and Logic can be boiled down to two simple rules for adults:

RULE #1:
Take care of yourself by setting limits in a loving way.

RULE #2:
Turn every mistake or misbehavior into a learning opportunity.

That's it. When we begin to experiment with these rules, we are on our way to becoming the best parents we can be— and also having a lot more fun with our kids. In this chapter and the next, we will learn more about Rule #1. In Chapter 6, we'll get better acquainted with Rule #2. Sit back, relax, and get ready for a life with lower blood pressure and happier, more responsible kids.

THE FIRST RULE OF LOVE AND LOGIC

Take good care of yourself by setting limits in a loving way.

- Replace anger and frustration with empathy.
- Replace threats and warnings with simple actions.
- Set limits you can enforce.
- Give away the control you don't need.

The first rule of Love and Logic parenting, with children of any age, is to set limits in a loving way. When we make a child aware of our limits, and do it in a caring way, we take good care of ourselves and model healthy behavior.

Discipline without Frustration or Anger

Many of us have been taught that we get kids to behave by angrily laying down the law. That's how some of our parents operated, and so did many of their parents before them. In the "good old days," these techniques often seemed to work. Have times ever changed! In today's society, parents are seeing over and over that anger and frustration actually make the problem worse. In fact, nothing seems to make a sour behavior stick better than an entertaining display of parental frustration and anger.

Isn't it amazing? After all this time, it turns out that getting frustrated and angry gets us the exact opposite of what we want. Take a look at Alex and his mother as they sit in the airport.

It's late in the evening, and four-year-old Alex is tired and bored. He and his mom are waiting for a commuter flight. He's saying, "I want to go to Grandma's *now*! I *hate* this place! It sucks!"

His mother is tired, too, and frustrated. She says, "You stop saying that! It's not nice! Cut that out! Stop it right now, young man!"

Alex pinches her. She responds immediately with more anger. "You *pinched* me? We don't *do* that! We treat each other with *respect* around here! That's one!" The kid continues to misbehave. "That's two!" his mother says. "Alex! Don't you do that again!" When he does, she takes him into the rest room and spanks him.

A minute later, Alex emerges from the bathroom with his mother. Snot is running out of his nose, and his face is red as a tomato. When they sit down again, Alex continues his meltdown. The more frustrated and angry mommy gets, the more monster-like Alex becomes.

Saved by the boarding announcement, Alex and his mother board the plane, which is half empty. They sit right behind a businessman who's reading. Within minutes, Alex starts to kick the back of this poor gentleman's seat.

The man turns around and calmly says to the mother, "Can you please do something about your child? He's kicking the back of my seat."

The pent-up and upset mother gives the man a look of exasperation and says, "What do you expect me to do?"

Ten minutes later Alex is still kicking away. Really irritated now, the man stands up and chooses a seat right behind Alex. Now the tables are turned, and this grown man is kicking the back of the boy's seat!

The mother turns around and says, "What are you doing?"

With all of the sarcasm he can muster, the businessman responds, "What do you expect me to do? I can't help it."

❤ ❤ ❤

The Misbehavior Cycle

It's easy to laugh at the story of Alex and his mommy because it's happening to somebody else. But wait! What if the tables are turned, and we are the ones in the parental hot seat? When a parent scolds and threatens a child, and the child continues to misbehave, what has the parent achieved? More important, what is this child learning? Here's what happens.

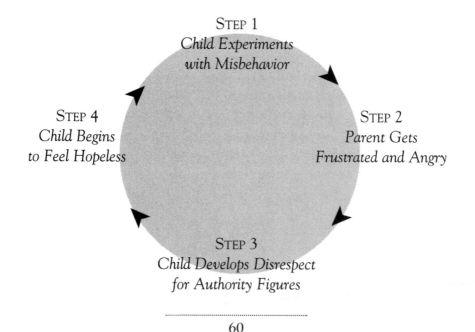

The Misbehavior Cycle

STEP 1
*Child Experiments
with Misbehavior*

STEP 2
*Parent Gets
Frustrated and Angry*

STEP 3
*Child Develops Disrespect
for Authority Figures*

STEP 4
*Child Begins
to Feel Hopeless*

THE MISBEHAVIOR CYCLE STEP #1:
Child Experiments with Misbehavior

Every child worth keeping is going to experiment with misbehavior. In fact, the healthiest little children are those who act like young scientists. These little Einsteins run experiments to see how the world works. They decide, based on analyzing the results of their research, how they want to live their lives. Part of their experimentation includes behavior we don't like. In their little subconscious minds, they seem to do a lot of pondering: "I wonder what would happen if..."

"I wonder what will happen if I spit food across the table." "I wonder what's going to happen if I lie down while I'm shopping with my mom and start to scream 'I *want* it. I *want* it!' " Some of the experiments are sour, and some are sweet. "I wonder what will happen if I say please or give Mommy a hug." "I wonder what will happen if I just sit here and quietly eat my food."

THE MISBEHAVIOR CYCLE STEP #2:
Parent Gets Frustrated and Angry

The best way to create a "mad scientist" rather than a marvelous one is to get really angry and frustrated when your child misbehaves. Remember, anger and frustration feed misbehavior. It's often easy to forget this and start the lectures, "Don't you do that! That's not nice. That's one! That's two! That's two and one-half! That's fifteen and three-quarters!"

Soon the child hears the dreaded parental, "I mean it!"—which actually says to the kid, "I'm totally out of skills, and I have no idea what I'm going to do with you!" No wonder kids often grin when they hear these words.

THE MISBEHAVIOR CYCLE STEP #3:
The Child Develops Disrespect for Authority Figures

Sadly, the child looks up at the adult and, on a subconscious level, begins to believe some rather unfortunate things:

• **"Wow! Look at this. The most powerful people in my life can't make me behave."** The child develops a perception of authority figures as easily frustrated and easy to push around. Sadly, this belief can last a lifetime and create major pain for everyone, particularly the child.

• **"Hey! It's really entertaining to see big people ticked off!"** Have you ever known people who've made a hobby out of frustrating their teachers, boss, police officers, or spouse? What a bummer! Just pray someone like this never buys the house next door.

THE MISBEHAVIOR CYCLE STEP #4:
The Child Begins to Feel Hopeless

How must a child begin to feel when nobody is able to make him or her behave in a loving way? Consider the following:

"If the most powerful people in my life can't make me behave, and they're all bigger and older than I am, I must be pretty bad—really bad and pretty hopeless."

Using anger and frustration is one of the quickest ways to make children develop a negative view of authority figures—and then, themselves. When kids feel bad about themselves, hopelessness soon follows—"Why should I even try when I'm so bad?"

**Self-concept equals behavior.
We act according to how we see ourselves.**

When kids feel good about themselves, the odds go up in favor of their behaving well. Think about it for a moment. Are you ever around someone who just plain believes in you? It rubs off on you, doesn't it? And don't you find that you're always your best around that person? Like us, kids rise to the occasion when they feel good about who they are.

In contrast, have you ever noticed what it's like to be around someone who's constantly critical? How do you act around them? Do you find yourself actually living *down* to their expectations? Do you ever find yourself giving them the very *worst* you have to offer?

Breaking the Cycle

How do we prevent or break the misbehavior cycle? Simply put, we show our kids that we can handle them without breaking a sweat. We replace anger and frustration with soft words and powerful yet kind actions.

If they can handle me that easy, I must be OK!

Let's take a look at how one Love and Logic parent proved this to his young son.

I (Charles) watched a father and son as they did a bit of shopping in our local grocery store. Let's call them Henry and Warren. Henry is toddling behind his father, Warren. Soon, Henry is gravitating toward everything on the shelf, "I want this. I want this. I want that." Before long, he's sitting in the middle of the aisle playing with objects he's pulled off the shelves.

Some parents might stop right there and say, "Stop that right now!" or, "You put that back on the shelf!" "Come on! Come on!" But Warren doesn't break a sweat. He just keeps moving and walks around the corner where Henry can't see him, but he can see Henry. Giggling as he peeks around the corner, Dad watches his sweet little boy.

Suddenly the air is pierced with screams, as Henry realizes that he might just be "lost." "Where's my daddy! Daddy!" he yells, running down the aisle. Seeing his son round the corner of the shopping aisle, Warren smiles and says, "Hey, Henry, little buddy! Good to see you again! I was wondering if you were going to catch up with me today. It's always a better day when you go home from the store with the same number of kids you started with." And he keeps moving.

What's Warren doing? Is he showing little Henry that he can handle him without breaking a sweat? What's Henry learning? He's learning his job—which is to keep up with Dad. Warren continues to whistle. Do actions speak louder than words?

❤ ❤ ❤

The rest of this book is dedicated to helping you discipline your kids without having to lose one excess drop of perspiration. Why was Warren's approach in the store so powerful? Simply because he replaced anger, frustration, and lots of words with one simple action—walking away.

When we do discipline without showing frustration, the odds for success increase in a very big way.

Love and Logic Experiment #4

Have Some Fun with Temper Tantrums

Tantrum-tamer #1: Keep on truckin'.

The next time your child has a tantrum in the store, keep on truckin'. That's right. Walk away, turn the corner, and peek around it. Make sure your child can't see you. Most kids will suddenly realize that you aren't going to hang around for their fits, and they'd better keep up.

For a fun example of this approach, review the story of little Henry on pages 63–64.

By the way, this same technique works at home too.

Tantrum-tamer #2: Encourage the art form.

A second strategy for taming tantrums is to encourage the art form. When your child begins a meltdown, put a bored look on your face and say, "Nice fit, but I think you are losing your touch. Last time you screamed a lot louder and kicked your feet a lot harder. I'm really disappointed. Show me how it's really done. Give me your best. Come on."

A friend of ours routinely used this approach with her son. With a smile on her face, she recounted one day when she begged her son to have a fit. How did he respond? With both hands on his hips and a twisted little face, he said, "No! I don't want to!"

CHAPTER FIVE

Give Your Children an Advantage in Life

The Way the Real World Works

Love and Logic is devoted to helping parents raise kids who are prepared for the real world. What does this mean? Like frustration and anger, which get us nothing but more of the same, threats and repeated warnings do not prepare our kids for real-life situations. I (Charles) got a strong grip on this concept as I drove to the airport one day.

Finally I had a car with less than 300,000 miles on the odometer! It even had a cassette player instead of an 8-track. Remember those? As I was speeding down the freeway, looking more at the cassette player than the road, I glanced up just in time to see a tire fly off of a truck and land right in front of me. What was I to do? I couldn't go left. I couldn't go right. I couldn't stop in time. All I could do was grit my teeth and hope for the best.

I pulled over to the side of the road and got out of the car. Quickly surveying the damage, I noticed oil all over the road. Then I saw the interesting collection of car parts decorating the highway behind me. What a drag! Immediately my brain began surging, "What do I do now? I'm going to miss my flight. Then

I'm going to miss my meeting in Omaha. Then I might lose my job." Luckily, I had my cell phone with me. Calling my office, I begged for a quick ride to the airport—and a tow truck.

It was a close call, but I actually made my flight. In my hotel room that night, I tried to get some sleep. As I closed my eyes, the inside of my eyelids became television sets. What did I see? The entire incident kept replaying itself over and over again in my head—the tire flying out of control, me hitting it, the oil on the road, my heart racing, etc. It occurred to me that there had to be a reason why this experience was burned so deeply in my subconscious mind. There had to be some reason why this event had such a great impact on me. All I knew at the moment was that I was never again going to watch the stereo more carefully than the road. Why will I never forget this lesson?

Is it because the accident happened so quickly? Was it because the experience was scary? Was it possibly because the tire came without warning? Suddenly I made this revelation. Kids are better prepared for real life when adults don't give repeated warnings! Why? Real-world consequences, and calamities, often happen without warning. Is it wise for us to prepare kids for this in advance?

Did a state trooper pull up alongside me as I was driving down the highway and yell, "You better not look at that cassette player while you're driving. You might get into an accident. Watch the road! That's one."?

Did he roll up his window, move on, and let me go? Did I then get stopped by a sheriff, a mile down the road, who warned, "I've been talking to the state trooper back there, and you haven't been paying attention! You better stop that right now! We really mean it this time. That's two!"?

Further down the road, did the chief of police drive up and say, "That's two-and-a-half! We really do mean it this time!"? Of course not!

❤ ❤ ❤

Real-World Consequences often Happen without Warning

Is it possible that we give kids a distorted view of cause and effect when we warn them two, three, or four times before enforcing a limit or providing a consequence? By giving them all these warnings, do we plant a seed in their minds that can make them reason, "I really don't have to worry much about making careful decisions, because nothing really bad is going to happen until I'm warned at least two times."?

> **Our children are better prepared for life when they understand that the consequences of poor choices can happen without warning.**

How might a child who's been raised with repeated warnings deal with peer pressure? If someone says, "Hey, let's go smoke this crack, or have sex, or rob a bank," what might this kid think? Sadly, it's quite probable that he or she might reason, "Well, something bad might happen, but not right away. In fact, I can probably smoke crack and have sex at least two times before anything bad really happens."

Today, we're finding employers who say they're having a terrible time with their workforce. More and more employees have to be told five or six times to do something before they do it. If they get reprimanded or fired, they say silly things such as, "You didn't warn me! You only mentioned this once. You didn't tell me not to watch TV during work hours."

Learning to Make Wise Decisions—the First Time

We want our kids to have two major thoughts about the decisions they make:

- "Life's pretty good. People are kind to me and meet my needs. But if I make a poor decision, something bad could happen, and I'd have no warning."

- "Every decision I make is important. I wonder how this one's going to affect the rest of my life?"

Kids who think in this way have a fighting chance against peer pressure. Spared threats and repeated warnings, they quickly learn to make wise decisions—the first time. Wouldn't it be nice if our kids could start learning this as soon as possible?

Set the Limit Once and Follow Through

Young parents sometimes use warnings because they love their kids and have read pop psychology books that tell them to do so. Love and Logic parents do not warn their children two, three, or four times before imposing a consequence. They set the limit once—and follow through with loving yet powerful actions.

Instead of saying, "Pick up your toys . . ." and then saying, "Oh, now, didn't I tell you to pick up your toys?" and then warning, "If you don't pick up your toys, I'm going to have to . . . ," the Love and Logic parent simply says, "Feel free to keep the toys you pick up!"

That's it. Once is enough. Then, when the toys are still there, the parent says, "Oh, how sad," picks up the toys, and doesn't return them until the child has earned them back by doing some small chores or helping the parent in some other way. Using this approach, how long is it going to take for the child to get really good at picking up toys? If we teach our kids that sad things can happen if wise decisions aren't made the first time, will they be happier and safer in the long run? One thing is certain. Their future bosses will love them . . . and so will their spouses!

Give your kids an advantage in life.
Set limits once and follow through
with loving actions instead of warnings.
Teach them how to make wise decisions the first time.

The most successful parents don't talk a lot with their kids about misbehavior. They don't spend time processing psychological thought or warning their kids that something bad will happen if they don't do what they're told. Great parents simply follow through with actions—in a very loving way.

How Do We, "Set the Limit Once?"

It's easy to *say*, "Set the limit once," but how do we actually do it? With very young kids who don't yet understand language, we don't waste our breath. Instead, we change their location. "Uh-oh. You're throwing your carrots instead of eating them? You must be done eating. Let's get out of your high chair right now. Up we go."

Or, we take away the offending object. "Uh-oh. You hit the dog with your toy truck? All gone!" We hide the truck. The truck's gone. But we don't spend time talking about it, lecturing, or warning. We simply take action, and move on.

At about sixteen months of age, my (Charles's) son began insisting that he do everything on his own. His prime goal was to be "big." All day long I'd hear him say things like, "No! *I* open the door!" "No, *me* eat!" "I put shirt on *myself!*" "No! *Me* flush poo-poo!"

Breakfast was one of the things he desperately wanted to do by himself and for himself. I decided that since I was going to be home, I would put an old, worn-out shower curtain on the floor, give him a bowl of warm mush and let him go at it. If he was going to drop any on the shower curtain, I could fling it out in the backyard afterward, and everyone would be happy, including the dog.

I thought to myself, "While he's eating on his own, I'll have time to go in the other room and shave. This is great!" As soon as my face was covered with messy lather, I heard the sound. What was it? Outrageous giggling and laughter flowed from the dining room.

Rushing into the dining room, what did I see? It was horrifying! There was little Marc, giggling like a wild man. There was Lady, the cocker spaniel, wearing a bowl of warm cereal as a hat.

Her long tongue licked away at the mess, and her short tail wagged like crazy. She was happy. Marc was happy. I was not happy! Have you ever had fantasies about the "behavior management" techniques you'd really like to use with your kids?

I took a deep breath and told myself what I would tell you. "Handle this kid without breaking a sweat. That's the main thing. Don't get angry. Show him that handling him is a breeze."

So, I looked at Marc and sang the "Uh-oh" Song. What's the "Uh-oh" Song? "Uh-oh! That is so sad. Looks like a little bedroom time." Then I swept him off to his room for a little "thinking time." If Marc had *accidentally* bumped his bowl off the table, then I probably would have gotten down on the floor with him and we would have cleaned up the mess together and moved on with life. No big deal. This, however, was clearly not an accident. Marc had recently taken up the fine art of food flinging. Like any self-respecting toddler, he was experimenting. What was his subject? "What if I turn my bowl upside down on the dog's head? How will my dog react? What will daddy's face look like?"

I put Marc down on the bed and said, "Marc, honey, you can come out of your room as soon as you're acting sweet. Do you need the door open, or shut?"

He answered me with lots of screaming and a teddy bear upside the head. In toddler talk this mean's "Daddy, I need my door shut." As I left, I kept saying to myself over and over, "Don't say a word. Keep your mouth shut." As I closed the door, I heard him scream, "Mommy! I want my Mommy!"

❤ ❤ ❤

How does a parent ensure that the door stays shut? Simple, common sense solutions are usually the best. We can remove the handle, turn the door around so the lock is on the outside, or stuff the top of the door with a towel that makes the door difficult to open. Of course, we remain just outside the door, carefully monitoring the situation. The basic rule of thumb is this: The child stays in the room until he or she is calm. Then we wait a minute or two, for ourselves.

When we finally go into that room, after the child is calm, and after giving ourselves that extra minute or so, what is the first thing we do? Simply give the child a hug and say, "Sweetie, I love you. That was so sad." Then we go on with your lives. Do not fall into the trap of lecturing the child about what was learned. Why? Because doing so in essence says to your child, "You're not very smart, are you? You can't figure this out by yourself. How sad."

Save Most of the Attention for Happy Times

Some parents ask, "Why do you use the room? Why don't you just put him in the corner or on a chair?"

The reason we use a room rather than asking a child to stay in the corner or on a chair is because many of us have a hard time doing this without a red face and lots of words. What often happens is the child will start talking, crying, or trying to leave, and the parent will go over and give the child too much pizzazz: "You stay there! Don't leave! I told you to stay put! I mean it." Remember: Anger and frustration feed misbehavior.

The best way to raise a chronically unhappy and poorly behaved kid is to make a habit of giving them a lot of attention or pizzazz when they are misbehaving.

The nice thing about the room is that you can take your child there, latch the door, stay right outside the room, and avoid a major control battle. The key is making sure that you don't say anything to your child through the door. Remember, wise parents give their kids plenty of attention when they are acting sweet and little or no attention when they are acting sour.

What message do we want to send our children? "Sweetheart, the way you get lots of attention in this house is by behaving and by being nice. The way you get no attention in this house is by throwing fits and acting nasty."

Steps for the "Uh-oh" Song

Since the "Uh-oh" Song is such a powerful tool with very young kids, we like to make sure we always teach it well. How about a review of the important "Uh-oh" Song steps? Parents who've mastered them always tell us how much happier their families have become.

1. Instead of making threats or giving warnings, sing, "Uh-Oh" and take action. Maybe you'll carry your child into the bedroom and say, "Looks like a little bedroom time." Or maybe you'll take away an offending object and say calmly, "All gone!" Whatever action you take begins with "Uh-oh!" Why? Because singing this simple song really communicates, "You are such a great kid, and I am such a great parent, that I can handle you without yelling, without frowning, and without stressing myself out. Parents also tell us that singing "Uh-oh" also helps them stay calm.

Please note. This technique is not for infants and very young children who are crying or acting out because they have a need that must be fulfilled. When a child has a basic need, meet it instead of punishing or ignoring the child! Remember the Trust Cycle? The "Uh-oh Song" is designed to limit children's wants, not deprive them of what they need.

2. Gently lead or carry your child to his or her room. Make the room safe ahead of time. Wise parents remove anything that they don't want broken.

3. Give your child a choice about the door. "Do you need the door shut, or open?" If a child comes out before she's ready, then shut the door and make sure that it stays shut. Turn the lock around. Put a towel on top of the door; wedge it tightly so she isn't strong enough to pull it open. Put a latch on the outside. Whatever's safe and easily done. Remember to stay just outside the door.

4. Say, "Feel free to come out when you're acting sweet." Don't let your child out until she's calm. Some kids need temporarily extended time limits. With some children, the first few times this technique is used, they will need to be in the room for more than an hour. It's okay if a parent checks from time to time, but a kid really needs to stay in there until she's ready to behave. Parents using this technique tell us that the time required begins to shorten very quickly if they remain consistent. They say things like, "The first couple of days were, really hard. Then she rarely needed to go to her room or spend much time there. It's great! What a different kid."

Most kids are smart enough to figure out that misbehavior doesn't pay. There may be an extended initial period of adjustment, but that behavior usually starts to fade out rather rapidly—as long as parents don't interact with a child while he or she is in the room. The best way to make this technique backfire is to use too many words.

5. Do not lecture or remind when your child is ready to come out. This is the time to give him or her a big hug and move on with your day. If your child acts up again in a few minutes, just sing "Uh-oh" and repeat the technique. Some kids require more than one or two trips when they're first learning about "Uh-oh." Don't sweat it. That's normal.

6. Have fun with your kids when they're behaving. In order for this technique to work, do you think it might be smart to have a lot of fun with your kids when they're behaving? Some kids love to go to their room because it gets them away from a nasty parent.

A simple trick of successful parenting is to have lots of fun with your kids when they're behaving well so they'll miss you when they go to their rooms.

Be silly with your kids. Have fun. Partake in the joy. Then, when they misbehave, all the fun shuts down. You're not angry and you don't yell, but you are very boring when their behavior turns sour. Teach them that a life of misbehavior is pretty dull.

What Parents Say about the "Uh-oh" Song

Love and Logic parents tell us that the "Uh-oh" Song works so well that they don't have to use it often. What's the best part? The joy of this tool, they often remark, is that they find themselves spending less time warning, lecturing, and reprimanding, and more time playing and having fun with their tots. Now, that's the hallmark of an effective technique!

In a wonderful handwritten letter sent to us, we learned about a child who was visiting a neighbor with his mother. Just as he began to misbehave, Mom looked down at him and sang, "Uh-oh." What happened? The child *immediately* stopped and asked, "Where am I supposed to go?" Mom merely responded, "Thanks for stopping! You can stay with us as long as you are acting sweet."

Lock in the "Uh-oh" Song at Home

Anything that works at home first has a better chance of working outside the home later. Psychologist types call this phenomenon the "transfer effect." The learning that takes place at home tends to "transfer" to other places. We always suggest that parents get the "Uh-oh" Song locked in at home before trying it in public. Once a child learns to go to his or her room at home—and stay there—he or she is much more likely to go to the corner in the grocery store—and stay there!

Success using a corner at a store happens only if your child has first been conditioned to listen to "Uh-oh" at home. When your little sweetie is acting not-so-sweet in the store, you may try "Uh-oh. This is so s[...] your child off to spend some time next to the canned vegetables.

Walk a small distance away from them, where you can watch them out of the corner of your eye while giving them little or no attention.

The "Uh-oh" Song is a powerful technique for setting limits with young children. Another fabulous tool is what we Love and Logic folks call the enforceable statement. Wouldn't it be great if your kids believed that everything you said was gold? Wouldn't it be nice if they listened to you the first time?

Turning Your Words to Gold: The Art of Enforceable Statements

"Sit still!" "Be quiet!" "Keep your hands to yourself." What's wrong with these statements? Have you ever found yourself telling a child to do something that you can't really make him do? How long does it take a kid to start testing and to realize that he can win the battle every time? Most kids learn very quickly that, short of physical restraint, we cannot *make* them be quiet. Similarly, most learn quickly that we can't *make* them sit still. And, most learn quickly that we can't *make* them keep their hands to themselves. Each time we tell our kids to do something that we really cannot make them do, we give away some of our power and a whole lot of our credibility.

What happens when a parent says to two kids fighting in the backseat of the car, "Quit fighting." If the two keep up their warfare, the parent looks powerless. Short of physically separating them, a parent cannot *make* two kids stop dueling. Insightful Love and Logic parents recognize this and avoid the trap by using enforceable statements. What's an "enforceable statement?" Simply stated, enforceable statements describe limits that we can actually enforce 100% of the time. Instead of saying, "Quit fighting," a Love and Logic parents says something like, "I charge two dollars a minute to listen to fighting in the car. Will you be paying me with chores, cash, or some of your toys?"

Turn Your Words into Gold:
The Art of Enforceable Statements

Unenforceable Statements	Enforceable Statements
"Hurry up! Get ready! We need to leave!"	"The car is leaving in ten minutes."
"Put your coat on!"	"I'd be happy to take you when your coat's on."
"Pick your toys up!"	"Hey! Feel free to keep the toys that you pick up."
"Eat! For crying out loud, eat! There are starving kids in China!"	"Dinner is served until seven. That's five minutes from now. See the clock? When the big hand reaches the top, that means dinner is over."
"Stop shouting! You make me crazy when you yell so loud!"	"I'll listen as soon as your voice is as calm as mine."
"Brush your teeth!"	"I give treats to kids who protect their teeth by brushing."

Getting Ready for Day Care—Without Enforceable Statements

Every parent of a young child complains about mornings. Have you ever been amazed by how long it takes to leave the house with a young child? Many parents find themselves being late to work and torn between a boss who complains about tardiness and a child who takes forever to get ready. Brandon was such a child. Here's how his mother used to handle the problem.

Brandon once believed that mornings are like the art of making fine wine—never rush it! His mom tried everything she knew. "Put your clothes on," she begged as she rushed to get herself ready. Fifteen minutes later, when she would check on Brandon, she'd see him with one sock on, his pants half on and his shirt unbuttoned. "Put your clothes on!" she'd repeat, six or seven times.

Finally, from sheer frustration, she'd run in and put Brandon's clothes on him. Then she'd sit him down with a nice hot bowl of oatmeal. In slow motion, stirring it, Brandon made sculptures as the cereal hardened. He was really quite artistically gifted.

"Eat it, Brandon! How many times do I have to tell you to eat your oatmeal! There are starving kids in Bosnia! You don't know how lucky you are to have that food! You eat it!"

About thirty minutes later, Brandon would typically whine, "It's cold."

At the end of her parental rope, Mom would say, "It wouldn't be cold if you'd just eat it when you get it! For crying out loud. I'll heat it up for you, but this is the last time!"

Finally, as they'd be getting ready to leave, Brandon's mom would ask, "Where's your coat?"

"I don't know," Brandon would whimper.

"Didn't I tell you to get your coat? Where is it? Hurry up!"

Getting Ready for Day Care—With Enforceable Statements

Thank goodness parenting does not have to be this hard. When I met this frustrated, exhausted mother, we talked about enforceable statements and how they could help her, especially in the morning.

The first thing she learned to say is, **"Breakfast is served until 6:30."** She showed Brandon what 6:30 looks like on a large clock. "When the big hand gets to where this smiley face sticker is on the clock, breakfast is over."

After these two sweet and simple sentences, Mom went into another room and bit her tongue. This was one of the hardest things she'd ever done—saying those words, only those words, and nothing more. She was accustomed to giving her lectures about starving children, eating food when it's hot, and how lucky we are to have food. But she didn't. Good job, Mom!

When 6:30 came along, she walked over to the table where Brandon was playing with his food, picked up his plate, and said with genuine sadness, "Breakfast is over."

Brandon immediately began to cry. "I'm going to be hungry!"

Mom bit her tongue and said nicely, "Hang in there, sweetheart." To enforce the lesson, she called Brandon's school the day before and told his teacher that she wasn't starving her son, but instead was doing a little Love and Logic training session. She also made sure that his teacher knew that he had had an opportunity to eat, but chose to miss it. And she said, "Please, do *not* give him a snack in the morning because you feel sorry for him."

Directly after removing his plate, Mom used another enforceable statement. **"Hey, Sweetie. I give treats to kids who protect their teeth by brushing after eating."** Then she kept her mouth shut again. Good job, Mom! Smart parents don't waste their breath with unenforceable statements like, "Brush your teeth. I said brush your teeth, Brandon. Did you hear me? I said to brush your teeth now!"

Brandon, looking a bit surprised, asked, "What if I don't brush my teeth?" Mom took another breath and calmly replied, "That would be sad. But try not to worry about it."

Will Brandon be inspired to listen to his mom when she uses enforceable statements like these? Yes! Why? Because they consist of meaningful words—words that Mom can back up with actions. Finally, as Brandon is standing in the kitchen in his superhero pajamas and bunny ear slippers, his mom tries another enforceable statement. **"The car is leaving in ten minutes."** Again, she bites her lip and says nothing. Great job, Mom!

When ten minutes go by and Brandon still doesn't have his clothes on, what does Mom do? She silently scoops up his clothes, puts them in plastic bag and picks up Brandon. Needless to say, guess who's yelling, "I'm not ready! I'm not dressed!"?

"No problem," says Mom. "Your clothes are in this bag. Time to leave." She carries Brandon to the car and off they go.

❤ ❤ ❤

Brandon's mother wrote us a letter. It ended with these words: "I only had to do this once. And the day care people still can't believe how fast he got dressed!"

Obviously, we don't recommend using this with your fifteen-year-old and, to the best of our knowledge, it doesn't work well on spouses! But for toddlers and preschoolers, parents keep telling us about its magic. From that day on, Brandon's mom made no more than three statements each morning:

- "Breakfast is served until 6:30."
- "I give treats to kids who protect their teeth by brushing after eating."
- "The car leaves at 7:00."

Many parents find that once they've tried enforceable statements, they never go back to their old ways. They get even more excited when they hear about the next Love and Logic technique. Are you ready for another powerful tool for setting limits without power struggles?

Provide a Healthy Sense of Control

In Chapter 1, we learned the four basic principles of Love and Logic. Remember the one about sharing control? Limits are always easier to set and to enforce when children feel a healthy sense of control. In contrast, limits almost never stick when people feel coerced. Remember King George of England and how he treated Colonial America? What a control freak! He prohibited settlers from buying land beyond a certain territory. He imposed taxes on colonists for services they never requested. He told them how to spend their money, where they could live, and what religion they were to follow. What happened? They rebelled! Do you know of any parents whose teens have rebelled for similar reasons? Is it possible that there would be no such thing as the United States of America if King George had known about Love and Logic?

People have interesting ways of regaining control when they feel it's been taken away. It's human nature. When people feel overly controlled, their subconscious minds create a menu of strategies for regaining this control. What's on this menu? Let's take a look:

- I'm going to "forget" what they told me to do.
- I'll do what they asked, but I'll do it my way.
- I'll break something while I do what they asked me to do.
- I'll do the exact opposite of what they asked me to do.

Starting even before their children can speak, wise parents give lots of choices on small issues that they, the parents, don't care much about. Control is like many other things in life—the more we give, the more we get. We never have any more love in our lives than we give to others. We never get any more respect from others than we give them. And, we never have much more money in our bank account than what we deposit in the first place. To make withdrawals, we must first make deposits. Such is the same for control. Wise parents give plenty of choices on small issues, so they can make "withdrawals" on large ones. Parents who share control in this way generally enjoy cooperative, responsible teens. Ironically, parents who spend most of their time controlling every aspect of their kid's lives, end up having very irresponsible, out-of-control, and rebellious kids.

When we've made plenty of deposits in the form of small choices, our children are much more likely to cooperate when we say something like, "Sweetie. I know you don't want to do this, but who has been getting to make most of the choices around here? You have. This time it's my turn. Thank you."

Know When to Give Choices

Sometimes, there's confusion among parents about how and when to give choices. Here are some guidelines:

1. Give 99% of choices when things are going smoothly.
When your child is behaving, and things are going really well, that's the time to give as many choices as you can. Turn this into a game for yourself. Ask yourself, "How many choices can I give the kids today? Let's have fun with this. If I give them each ten choices, can I pull my weight when it's time for bed?"

Build up a "control bank account," so when you're feeling awful, you're sick, and the kids are acting up, you can say, "Honey, don't I usually give you a lot of choices? Well, today, since I feel bad, this is what I want." You don't have to feel guilty about it, and the odds are that your child will do it for you.

2. Provide choices only on issues that are not dangerous and don't create a problem—for anyone else on the planet.
Choices might include a selection of vegetables you've made for dinner; reading a favorite story or a new story before bedtime; picking up toys now, or in two minutes. If anyone could be hurt by a choice, it's not one to offer your child. Wise parents *do not*

say, "Honey, would you like to hold my hand as we cross the street, or would you rather run out in front of a car and get flat?"

3. Always offer two options, each of which makes you happy. Most parents learn quickly not to give choices such as, "Would you like to have carrots tonight, or Twinkies?" The smart choice is, "Would like to have carrots tonight, or broccoli?"

4. If the child does not choose in ten seconds flat, choose for the child. "What would you like tonight, milk or juice?" When your child hesitates longer than ten seconds or whimpers, "I want soda," you quickly respond, "Looks like juice." And you pour it.

Guidelines for Giving Choices

- Give 99% of choices when things are going smoothly.
- Provide choices only on issues that are not dangerous and don't create a problem for anyone else on the planet.
- Always offer two options, each a choice that makes you happy.
- Choose for the child in ten seconds flat if the child doesn't.

Although his parents don't use Love and Logic, Harry is a sweet little kid. He and Alex, both about five, were watching a movie one evening when Alex was having a sleepover. Alex's dad is a Love and Logic master. Here's what happened as it was getting close to bedtime.

"Okay, guys, time for bed," Alex's dad says.
"We haven't finished our movie," Harry replies.
"Yeah, Dad," Alex concurs with his buddy.
"Oops!" Dad says. "I forgot to give you a choice. Would you like to go to bed now, or would you like to go to bed when the movie's over in fifteen minutes?" Dad was clearly fine with either choice.

"We want to wait!" the boys cry in unison.

"Okay," says Dad. "Go ahead and wait."

When the movie is over, Dad asks, "Okay, guys, you want a story first, or no story?"

"A story!"

"Great. Okay. Do you want to hear about this turtle who didn't want to go to school, or do you want to hear about Muffin, the kitty who thinks he's a dog?" Finally, "You guys have to decide where you're going to brush your teeth. Do you want to brush them upstairs, or downstairs in the utility room with that cool sink?"

The beauty of these choices is that little children love them. They make these choices excitedly and feel they've gained some control in their lives. As an adult, you're thinking, "Is this silly, giving them these choices that don't seem to matter?" No way! Young children adore them.

"Okay, you guys, would you like a glass of water near your bed, or do you want to come to the sink anytime you get thirsty?" Then, "Do you want to sleep in bed, or do you want to pull all the covers onto the floor and pretend you're camping? Wouldn't that be cool? Well, you decide."

Finally, "Do you want your light on, or off?" This, Alex's dad decides, is the last choice he will give. Has Dad made a lot of deposits so far? No doubt. Now, it's his turn. "Okay, you two. It's time for bed."

"No! No! We don't want to go to bed. We're not tired!"

"Hey, don't I give you a lot of choices? Didn't you just decide . . ." and Dad runs down the list. Then, with great love in his eyes, he says, "Well, this last choice is mine. Time for bed. See you in the morning."

❤ ❤ ❤

In the morning, at bedtime, and in those moments kids have temper tantrums—when we set limits in a loving way, we can take potentially frustrating times and turn them into happy ones. That's what the magic of Love and Logic is all about.

Love and Logic Experiment #5

Hassle-Free Mornings

Review the three enforceable statements used by Brandon's mom.

Parents all over the country comment on how frustrating it can be to get their young kids ready for day care or school in the mornings.

Review the story of Brandon on pages 79–81. His mother used the following statements to save herself—and him—a world of grief:

- "Breakfast is served until 6:30. This is what 6:30 looks like on the clock."
- "I give treats to kids who protect their teeth by brushing."
- "The car leaves at 7:00. This is what 7:00 looks like on the clock."

Practice them over and over again in the shower.

Practice these statements over and over again in the shower, while driving to work, each night just before you fall asleep, or any other time you are alone and have some time to think.

Have a Love and Logic morning with your kids.

After you've practiced and feel confident, try this approach one morning. Once again, review Brandon's story to see how his mom pulled it off.

Remember: Actions speak louder than words. Set the limit once and follow through. For example, if your child fails to finish breakfast on time, lock in the empathy, remove his or her plate, and avoid the lectures.

Call your child's day care or school and let them know what you are doing and why. Ask them to avoid lecturing your child or rescuing him or her by providing extra snacks before lunch.

Pack a bag with an extra set of your child's clothes and place it by the door.

If your child continues to procrastinate, point at the bag and ask very calmly, "Sweetie, would you like to go to school with your clothes on your body or your clothes in a bag?"

If your child still doesn't get dressed, grab the bag and head for the car. What's the good news? Most parents only have to do this once!

CHAPTER SIX

Turning Misbehavior into Wisdom

Empathy Opens the Mind to Learning

In Chapters 4 and 5, we learn Love and Logic Rule #1: **Take care of yourself and set limits in a loving way.** We now know what this rule means. Rather than get angry or use threats and warnings, we set limits once, make statements we can enforce, give kids a healthy sense of control, and use meaningful actions instead of too many words.

An essential partner to that rule is Love and Logic Rule #2: **Turn every mistake or misbehavior into a learning opportunity.** How can parents make this happen? Simply stated, always give a strong dose of sadness or empathy *before* delivering a consequence. As we will show, this simple action can make the difference between a child who learns wisdom from the consequence and one who merely has a "meltdown" of anger, frustration, or resentment. Loving sadness, provided before the "bad news," opens a child's heart and mind for learning. Anger, in contrast, creates a child who blames others for his or her mistakes.

LOVE AND LOGIC RULE #2 FOR PARENTS:
Turn every mistake or misbehavior into a learning opportunity.
- Always provide a strong dose of empathy *before* delivering a consequence.
- Replace punishment with logical consequences.
- When possible, guide your child to solve his or her own problem.

Why Empathy?

The following story concerns two children who committed the same misbehavior at the same time. Their mothers, however, handled the situation quite differently. One scolded her child; the other used empathy, followed by consequences.

Notice, as you read the story, how the children react to their mothers' responses—what they do, what they say and what they learn. You may also consider which mother will have the most energy and enthusiasm at the end of the day.

Melissa and Rodney were painting watercolors for their mothers while the mothers visited over coffee and muffins. When their moms walked into the garden for a minute, the three-year-old budding artists decided to surprise their mothers with a beautiful painting—on the dining room wall. Oh, the joy of parenthood.

When Maria and Ginger returned and saw what their kids had done, their responses were immediate, but distinct.

"Rodney!" Ginger shouted. "You know better than to paint on a wall in someone's house! You're going to clean that off right now!" Rodney's proud smile quickly turned into a frown, and he started to cry. Soon an all-out temper tantrum erupted, complete with foot stomping and screaming. Ginger found it impossible to get him to stop.

Maria was angry, too, but she took a deep breath, calmed herself inside, and said, "Melissa, this is so sad. It's not okay to paint on the wall." In a kind voice she continued, "What are you going to do to fix this?"

"But, Mommy," Melissa said, "we wanted to give you a present."

"Thank you, Sweetie." She gave Melissa a hug as she and Melissa looked over at Rodney, who was still screaming and throwing his arms in every direction.

"What do you think you should do about this painting on the wall?" Maria asked Melissa with a whisper. "Even though it's really beautiful, paint goes on paper, not on the wall."

Melissa shrugged her shoulders and mumbled, "Don't know, Mommy."

"Can you put the wall in the dishwasher, or should you wipe it off with a towel?" her Mom asked.

Melissa's eyes lit up. "The wall's too big to put in the dishwasher, Mama. But Rodney and I can wipe it off. Then we can make another picture—just like it—on this paper! So you can still have a present!"

❤ ❤ ❤

Did you notice how the empathy worked here? Rodney self-destructed, whereas Melissa was able to think about what she had done and solve the problem with help from her mom. Both parents applied consequences—one with anger, one with empathy.

Maria handed the problem back to her daughter by asking, "What do you think you should do?" Because Melissa had no clear solution, Mom offered her a choice. Talk about sharing control and thinking! Melissa was not too young to pick the solution. It's highly likely that Rodney, given empathy instead of a scolding, would have done so, too.

Which mother do you suppose is typically happier at the end of each day? Which is more exhausted? Which does more arguing? Which parent has energy in the evening to enjoy adult time? We believe in this technique so much that we have to repeat it over and over. Empathy, empathy, empathy. It's the spoonful of sweet sadness that helps the medicine of learning go down.

Empathy—The Most Important Love and Logic Technique

Providing empathy before delivering consequences has a number of benefits. It preserves the parent–child relationship—no one has to shout, or shout back, in defense. Empathy allows your kids to think more about their mistake and less about being angry with you. Empathy forces your children to "own" the pain of their mistakes, rather than blaming this pain on you. And, very importantly, empathy decreases the chances of "paybacks" or revenge.

$$\text{Consequences + Anger = More Anger}$$
$$\text{Empathy + Consequences = Learning}$$

What Empathy Accomplishes
- Preserves the adult–child relationship.
- Prevents resentment and the chances of "payback" behavior.
- Models, and, therefore, teaches respect.
- Helps a child stay focused on what can be learned from a mistake, rather than on the adult's anger.

By using empathy, we model respectful behavior for our child. Our child learns that this is how to behave—that respect is important and is a valued, responsible way to live. Do you suppose your children, as a result, will be more likely to use empathy with you fifty years from now when the tables may be turned?

I (Charles) am now very thankful for being raised with Love and Logic. As a child and teenager, I wasn't always sure.

When I was about sixteen years old, some friends came over to my house on a regular basis. I suppose they came over to be with me, but sometimes I think they came over to be with my parents. "Your mom and dad are so cool," they would say. "They never yell. They never nag you. They're like Mr. and Mrs. Rogers!"

How did I respond? "Oh, you think it's so great to live around here with them. Ha! All they do is walk around and say things like, 'Oh, bummer' or 'What are you going to do?' I wished they'd just yell at me and get it over with."

Now that I am older, and I hope a bit wiser, I see the great wisdom in my parents' ways. Maybe this is why I still enjoy being around them!

❤ ❤ ❤

We Aren't Born with Empathy

A while ago, while we were presenting a Love and Logic conference, a woman piped up in the middle of our presentation and yelled, "'Tain't natural!" Dazed and confused, we asked her what she meant. What was her response? "'Tain't natural to be so nice to a kid when you feel like ringing her neck! What I feel like saying to my child is, 'Young'un! I brought you into this world, and I can take you right out!'"

What's the truth here? She's right—not about taking the kid out, but about the fact that empathy doesn't come naturally for most of us. It doesn't feel natural many times to be sad rather than angry when our kids act up. How can we make it easier for ourselves? How can we make if feel more "natural"? Let's take a look.

Keep It Simple!

In the last ten years, we've made a major discovery. The most powerful Love and Logic parents do not get complicated with their empathy—they don't use a variety of ways to dispense it.

They pick one empathetic response—one that suits them and their personality—and they stick with it, the same sentence, over and over again. Select one from the chart below or come up with one of your own. Find one that is easy to use, feels pretty natural, and fits your personality.

Quick Empathetic Responses
- "Uh-oh."
- "This is so sad."
- "Bummer."
- "Oh . . . that's never good."
- "How sad."

Why use only one? Using the same words of empathy in every situation makes learning easier for both the child and the parent. For adults as well as kids, it's easier to remember. It's that simple. The goal here is to learn one quick and easy strategy so we can deliver empathy even when we're angry, frustrated, or downright dumbfounded. Some parents we've known repeat their chosen response over and over again every night before they go to bed. Why? So it becomes a permanent and automatic part of their life. Others achieve this by writing it down on little notes and sticking them all over their house, car, and office. I visited one friend who had little yellow notes all over her house saying, "Bummer." Are you guessing this piqued the interest of more than one visitor to her home?

I (Charles) will never forget a little boy who taught me the power of using just one simple, empathetic phrase.

He was about seven years old when he came to a Love and Logic event with his parents. Out of his earshot, his mother whispered to me, "We adopted him, and he was really out of control."

I said, "But he's not now?"

And she said, "We've been using this Love and Logic stuff on him, and it's been working great."

This little guy was so cute, I couldn't resist the urge to walk over and talk to him. I noticed that he had a little bandage on his knee. Have you ever noticed how young kids love to talk about their "owies"? One of the best ways to bond with little kids is to comment on their wounds. I've also noticed this working the same way with adult males. Remembering this, I asked, "Hey, wow! How did you get that boo-boo?"

The story was long and full of exciting detail. As it unfolded, I learned how he had fallen off of his bike, how his mom had kissed it, and how it still hurt just a bit. Trying to be a sympathetic listener, I said, "What a bummer."

Suddenly, he stepped back and opened his eyes very wide. He looked at me, and in an instant I could read his mind. It was as if he was asking, "What did I do?"

His mother, watching the whole thing, looked over at me, held in a laugh, and whispered, "Oh! We save 'bummer' for special times."

Right then and there, I realized that I had accidentally mumbled this child's cue, the single empathetic response his parents had used over and over before delivering discipline.

❤ ❤ ❤

Empathy + Consequences:
Kids Younger Than Three

There are two main patterns for using empathy and consequences with young children, and they are both easy to learn and use. When tikes younger than age three experiment with misbehavior—throw their bottle, pull a sibling's hair, bite, spit, or kick—use the following three steps.

Three Steps to Empathy + Consequences: Children Younger Than Three Years of Age

When your child misbehaves:

- Respond with empathy.
- Change your child's location or remove the "offending" object—or both.
- Don't warn, lecture, or remind. Let actions speak louder than words.

- First, use the empathetic response you've chosen—"How sad" or "What a bummer" or "Oh, that's never good."

- Second, either change your child's location or remove the "offending" object—or both. The bottle he was using to hit the dog, for example, is taken away, and your child is put in the crib.

- Third, allow the consequence to do the teaching. Warnings, lectures, reminders merely feed the problem. Actions speak louder than words.

Parents Who Use This Formula

Many parents we've met across the country use this simple method with their young children. What do they say about it? Almost all of them comment on how much better it works than trying to reason with their children. They also describe how fast their children learn to stop misbehaving as soon as they hear simple statements, such as "Uh-oh" or "How sad." Once again, parents are left with more time to have fun with their kids.

Remember the child in chapter one? The child who waddled over to the staircase while his family was eating to test the "no stair-climbing" rule? He started up the stairs, his mom said "no," he started to climb, and Mommy sang, "Uh-oh." *That was step one.*

Next, she picked him up and brought him to the table, changing his location. He was forced to sit on the floor, between her legs while she ate. She remembered to do this without repeated warnings or anger. *That was step two.*

Junior did not thank Mommy for her new technique. Instead, he threw a major fit. What did Mom do? She simply held him there until he was calm. *That was step three.* Afterward, when Junior grew calm, his mommy hugged him, and they all moved on.

Here's another example.

♥ ♥ ♥

An adorable little girl named Britt had a favorite television show and a favorite character she regarded as her "buddy." One afternoon, her daddy wanted to catch the news for a special report. When he told her he was going to watch the news instead of her buddy, Britt began to scream at the top of her lungs, "I want my buddy! I want my buddy! I want my buddy!"

"Uh-oh," her father said and picked her up. "Uh-oh," he repeated. "Looks like a little bedroom time." Off they went to Britt's bedroom, where she stayed until she calmed down. Did her dad talk with her while she was in the bedroom? No. Did he stay near her room to make sure she was okay? Yes. Did he remember to keep his mouth shut and avoid lecturing? Yes. And when she finally came out—a sweeter, kinder Britt—did he give her a simple hug and say, "I love you."? Yes! Way to go, Dad!

Britt's dad missed most of the news that afternoon. He gave it up for an opportunity to teach Britt an important lesson. Love and Logic parents are rumored to do such things. Are you guessing that Britt is going to be a more pleasurable teen to be around someday as a result?

Shari and Gloria are two caring moms who have very young toddlers. Take a look at both of them as they talk to their young kids. When Shari talks to her nine-month-old baby, listen to the words she uses, her tone of voice, and her expectations.

Shari's Orders

"Open up! Wider. Eat *all* of this! No! Don't spit it out! I said, no, *don't* spit. You have to eat your peas. They're *good* for you. Now don't turn your head. I said, open *up*. . . . Quit spitting! Eat your food! You are going to be hungry!"

Shari's commentary consists of *orders* or unenforceable statements. This kid is also too young to really understand what she's really saying. All her baby sees is a furrowed eyebrow, a downturned mouth, and a person who's fussing over every action. By the time Shari's child understands English, might her child believe that such commands are meaningless? Shari is training her child to believe that her orders mean nothing. She's also modeling bossy, irritable, and impatient behavior. Do we need to have a moment of silence for Shari when this child becomes a teenager? What comes around goes around.

Now, take a look at Gloria, whose baby is also nine months old. Notice how she uses the simple empathy and consequences pattern.

Gloria's Observations

"Whew!" she says. "Oh, you really want to spit food today. This is so sad. Looks like lunch is over." She removes the food from her child's high chair and takes him to his playpen.

When Gloria's child misbehaved, she used her empathetic response, "This is so sad." That's step one. Secondly, she took the food away from her child and changed his location. That's step two. Lastly, she let actions speak louder than words. That's step three.

What was most important here? She set limits and followed through with loving actions. No anger. No Warnings. No lectures. No Reminders.

**Show your children you can handle them
without breaking a sweat.**

It's All about Love and Hope

Did you notice how each Love and Logic parent avoided anger and frustration? Did you see how they showed their kids how they can handle them without breaking a sweat? When we can do discipline this easy, we show our kids great love, and we give them hope. It's as if they begin to reason, "If my parents can handle me this easy, I must be a pretty great kid!"

With three simple steps, many parents have changed their lives and taught their tots memorable lessons. You can do it, too. For those of you who have kids over the age of three, this simple approach often continues to work well. In fact, I know a mother who used it on her teenager. How? After she caught him abusing the family car by burning rubber and driving recklessly, she locked in the empathy, changed the "location" of his set of keys, and kept her mouth shut. Although this didn't win her heaps of gratitude from him, her car stayed in one piece and the neighborhood streets were once again safe.

**Love and Logic parents look forward to their children's
misbehavior. Why? The path to responsibility and wisdom
is paved with mistakes.**

Love and Logic Experiment #6

The Power of Empathy

Pick just one empathic phrase you can use with your kids.

Listed below are some examples used by parents across the country:

"How sad."

"What a bummer."

"This sure must hurt."

"Oh ... something like this never feels good."

"I love you. This must be hard."

Choose one of these or make up your own.

Remember to avoid sarcasm.

Sincere empathy works wonders. Sarcastic empathy results in resentment.

Practice your single empathic statement over and over.

Write the phrase over and over again on little sticky notes. Put them all over the house where you will see them throughout the day.

Say your phrase over and over again in the shower, while you are driving, right before you fall asleep at night, etc.

Visualize or imagine yourself using this phrase with your kids. Visualize yourself staying calm and being sincere.

Use this same response each and every time you have to give a consequence.

Parents often comment that this simple tool makes a world of difference with their kids. There is nothing quite like sincere empathy to build and preserve loving parent–child relationships.

CHAPTER SEVEN

Give Them the Gift of Thinking

Building Responsibility and Self-Esteem

Wouldn't it be great if, at the end of the day, your kids went to bed more tired from thinking than you? When children reach age three or so, the fun can really begin. How? When our kids misbehave or make mistakes, we can start asking them, "How are you going to solve this problem?" There is nothing more fun than watching the smoke come out of a child's ears as they think. And, there is nothing that builds responsibility and self-esteem faster than giving them just a bit of guidance and allowing them the satisfaction of looking back and saying to themselves, "I did it!" Thinking is just like any other skill—practice makes perfect.

Families are always happier when parents solve their own problems—and their children do the same.

When a very young child starts to cry in a store because she doesn't get what she wants, it is best for a parent to use the simple "empathy + consequences" formula that we learned in the previous chapter. Clearly, there is no benefit in asking a one-year-old, "How are you going to solve this problem?" In contrast, with a child approximately three years or older we might experiment with handing the problem back in a loving way. What do we mean?

Come and meet little Marc and his father. As we eavesdrop on their shopping trip, we'll get a glimpse of how Love and Logic parents hand problems back while teaching their children about the real world.

Marc, who's almost four, often goes with his father to a drug-store. This store carries everything—including toys. Whenever they go, the toy aisle—like a black hole in space—sucks him in. He gravitates toward cars, trucks, and other objects he can pull off the shelves. Playing with them is so much fun!

Much to the chagrin of his father, we see little Marc drawn to the most forbidden toy in his household—the bow and arrow set with suction cups. His father thinks to himself, "No way! I'll have those things stuck on my forehead, on the cat, on the fine china, all over the house. No way!" Dad has some choices to make. One option might be to say something like, "Put that back on the shelf. What do you think? Do you think that money grows on trees? Besides, you're gonna put your eye out with that thing!"

Instead, his father takes a deep breath, remembers his Love and Logic training, and makes another decision. His son is old enough to do some thinking on his own. He waits until they stand in the long check-out line. Then he looks down at his son, smiles, and asks very sincerely, "How are you going to pay for that?"

His son whines, "What? I don't know. You're going to buy it for me!"

What is Dad's response? He whispers, "This is so sad."

Marc immediately thinks, "Oh no. It's that 'This-is-so-sad' thing!"

Dad continues, "Would you like some ideas?"

Marc whimpers, "What?"

"Some kids decide to feel around in their pockets and see if they have any money. How would that work?"

"I don't have any money!" Marc complains.

"That's sad," Dad responds, "Would you like another idea?"

"Yes," Marc whines.

"Well," says Dad, "some kids decide to put it back on the shelf and wait until they are older and have some money. How would that work?"

Marc is unhappy and feisty. "I want it now! I want it!"

"I just have one more idea, but I'm not sure it's a good one. Some kids decide to take it out of the store and risk getting in big trouble. How would that work?"

"Oh, that's a good idea. I'm taking it!" Marc says, believing he's found the perfect solution.

Standing just behind Marc and his dad are two tough-looking guys who've been listening to the conversation and grinning all of the time. One of them turns around and says very seriously to the boy, "Yeah! Then the cops come and take you away."

Marc's eyes get really big, but he isn't ready to give in. Dad smiles down on him and says, "I'll love you no matter what happens. Good luck."

When they reach the counter, what do you suppose happens? Marc, like any other self-respecting kid, puts the bow and arrow set right on top of his father's purchases. Dad moves it off to the side, looks at the check-out lady, and says, "This cute little boy here is my son. He's going to talk to you about how he's planning to get this bow and arrow set out of the store without paying for it. I'll let you guys take care of that after I pay for my things."

In a second, without a word, Marc runs back to the toy aisle and returns the bow and arrow set to where he first grabbed it.

Walking back, he says to his father, "I hate you! You would've bought it for me if you were nice." How does his father respond? With a big, loving hug, Dad whispers, "I know it's hard." As they drive away from the store, Marc is already getting over his anger. He and his father enjoy the rest of the day. As we say at the Love and Logic Institute, "Empathy soaks up emotions."

♥ ♥ ♥

Who did the most thinking here? Sweet little Marc did the lion's share. Is he now becoming better prepared for life? The trick here is to ask lots of questions instead of telling your child what to do.

Questions cause children to think.
Commands cause children to resist.
Love and Logic parents choose thinking over resistance any day!

Helping Kids Solve Their Problems

Marc's father used five steps to help his son own and solve the problem. The first step is locking in the empathy. Marc's dad said, "That is so sad." Then, he asked, "How are you going to pay for that?" Asking your child how they plan to solve the problem is step two. When Marc responded, "I don't know," Dad asked "Would you like some ideas?" That's step three. By asking these questions, Dad accomplished at least two important things. First, he let Marc know that the problem belongs to Marc. Secondly, he sent the following message: "Son, you are capable!"

Five Steps for Helping Kids Own and Solve Their Problems

- Lock in the empathy.
- Ask your child, "What are you going to do?"
- When your child says, "I don't know," ask, "Would you like to hear some ideas?"
- Offer no more than three possible solutions. After each one ask, "How would that work for you?"
- Allow your child to choose—and learn from the choice and your empathy.

"How Would That Work for You?"

Marc's dad gave him some possible solutions to his problem. After each one, he asked, "How would that work for you?" That's step four. Marc was allowed to choose, and learn from his choice. Love and Logic parents actually hope for poor choices. Why? We keep saying it! The road to responsibility and wisdom is paved with mistakes. Is it best for children to make poor choices early in life, when the price tags of the consequences are low? Or is it best for them to make them later, when the price tags are very high—in possibly life-or-death situations? Will Marc be happier and more responsible in the long run if he first learns about the consequences of stealing at age three or at age twenty-three? Poor choices clearly become more costly with age!

"I'm Having an Energy Drain"

Parents everywhere we go describe the handiness of this five-step approach. Some offer very creative, and amusing, applications. When children misbehave, it's not uncommon to find oneself at a loss for the type of consequence to provide. One mother we met described how she uses the five steps to provide a "generic" consequence. Apparently, her first experiment with it took place when her child began getting into the nasty habit of lying to her. Catching her young son shading the truth, she very theatrically declared, "What an energy drain!" Then she said, "This is so sad. When you lie, it drains my energy. How are you going to put it back?"

Dazed and confused by her display, he simply muttered, "Don't know." Then, she asked him, "Do you want some ideas?"

"Ok," was the only response he could muster.

"Well, some kids decide to clean the toilet. That puts energy back into Mom. Some kids decide to go out and clean the backyard. That puts energy back. Some kids decide to vacuum. That's an energy builder. How would one of those work for you?"

"I don't know how to do that stuff," he replied.

"Not to worry," she answered, "I'll show you how to get started. Which would you like to do?"

"Vacuum. I want to vacuum."

Telling us this story, Mom laughed as she described what he looked like as he was pushing and pulling the sweeper around the living room. Too short to easily reach the handle, he stood on his tiptoes, grabbed it, and pulled it down. As a result, the bottom of the sweeper flipped up, and he ended up vacuuming more air than carpet. Caution! Wise parents never criticize their young children when chores are not done absolutely perfectly. The more we criticize when they are little, the more they will resist doing chores as teens...and spouses! Instead, smart moms and dads say things like, "Wow! You worked hard. Thanks."

After vacuuming part of the living room, he looked up at her and asked, "Am I done yet? This is really hard."

In a feeble tone of voice, holding her hand up to her forehead, Mom answered, "I still feel weak...very little energy. Try some more. You're getting close."

After finishing the room, he asked again, "Am I done yet?"

Mom responded with a somewhat stronger voice, "I'm feeling much better. I bet all of the energy will be back after you finish the hall."

How did he respond? "But I'm tired."

What did she say? "I know."

Finally, just as he finished the hall, she proclaimed with great excitement, "I'm feeling much more energetic. Thank you! Give me a big hug. You did it!"

When this mother first used the "energy drain" technique, she was concerned. Why? Her son seemed to be happy afterward. Aren't kids supposed to cry and be visibly upset after being disciplined? Not necessarily! Some of the best discipline occurs when both the parent and the child feel good afterward. The parent feels good, because the child has worked hard and repaid his or her debt to society. The child feels good, because he or she feels a sense of accomplishment and self-respect.

Every opportunity to own and solve a problem enhances a child's self-respect.

We are always amazed at how long children can remember the lessons they learn from techniques like the "energy drain." A dad heard the story you just read. Giving it a try, he found that it had worked quite well with their only child, Kevin. When Kevin started whining in the store, Dad would remark, "Oh no! Energy drain." When Kevin left toys on the floor for Mom and Dad to fall over, Dad would remark, "Oh no! Energy drain." When Kevin threw fits at the dinner table, Dad would remark, "Oh no! Energy drain." As you may have guessed, Kevin became very good at doing chores to put energy back into his parents. His mother even remarked, "I started looking forward to him acting up so I could get some extra chores done."

Before long, Kevin made a decision, "I'm sick and tired of putting energy back into my parents!" What happened then? He started acting really nice and responsible most of the time. What a bummer! Why? Now Mom and Dad had to do their own chores!

Kevin had become so well behaved that his parents hadn't had a real energy drain for about two years. In the mean time, his baby sister, Kristin, was born. As Kristin became a toddler, she and Kevin began to develop a nasty habit of arguing very loudly in the backseat of the car. What did Dad try? "Uh-oh! Energy drain."

It had been over two years since Kevin heard this. How did he react? With eyes wide, he turned to his sister and said, "Stop fighting! Dad's gonna make us do chores!"

❤ ❤ ❤

Kevin's father was amazed that Kevin, after all of that time, remembered the meaning of "energy drain." It was proof to him that young children can learn and remember a lot more than we often believe they can. He and his wife were also very amazed at how this simple tool lowered their daily worry and stress levels.

"We used to worry that we wouldn't know what to do when our kids acted up. This trick works in so many different situations that we rarely find ourselves wondering, 'Oh great. What do we do now?'"

What to Do When "Energy Drain" Doesn't Seem to Fit

The energy drain is a wonderfully powerful and flexible tool. But what's a parent to do if the child becomes so resistant that they refuse to put energy back? What's a parent to do when the energy drain technique just doesn't seem to fit the problem? That's when many parents find themselves at a loss for what to do. All of us have been there! All of us have found ourselves wondering, "Oh, great. Now what do I do?" Love and Logic teaches a fun and effective way of handling such situations. Let's take a look at a mother who tried it out.

Little Jenny was riding in the car with her mother and father one sunny Saturday afternoon. Heading for Grandma and Grandpa's they were all having a good time. That is, they were having a good time until Jenny spotted the sign of one or her favorite fast-food spots. Has it ever amazed you how quickly kids can spot the "golden arches" from the backseat of the car?

"Daddy!" she cried. "Let's stop! I want a toy meal! I want a toy meal! I want a toy meal!"

Mom answered, "We'll stop there some other day, sweetheart. We're going to have a nice dinner at Grandma and Grandpa's house."

In the rearview mirror, Mom could see Jenny turning beet red. Her sweet, angelic child became silent for just a moment, took a deep breath, and yelled, "Mommy, you're a butthead!"

Delaying Consequences Gives Us Time

Oh boy! Are you guessing that Mom is just a bit upset? Absolutely! Are you guessing that she is all ready to lock in the empathy and deliver a consequence? No way! Many of us have heard from "experts" that parents need to provide an immediate consequence when a child has an outburst like this. In reality, how many parents are really good at coming up with perfectly logical consequences, delivered with empathy, when they are in the middle of driving, shopping, or talking on the telephone and their kids have just made them really mad?

Let's get real here. No matter how many parenting skills we have, it's almost impossible in many situations to deliver an appropriate consequence when we're feeling angry, overwhelmed, or perplexed. Give yourself a break! When you're exhausted, overwhelmed, undecided about what to do—delay the consequence. What does this mean? Let's take a look at how Mom dealt with little Jenny's new vocabulary word.

Hearing "Mommy, you're a butthead" does not fill a parent with joy. Mom was beginning to have thoughts about the parenting techniques she'd really *like* to use, when she remembered to stay calm and use the delayed consequence.

What did she do? What does the delayed consequence sound like. Glancing at Jenny in the rearview mirror, Mom said, "This is so sad. Dad and I are going to have to do something about what you said, but not now. Later." Taking a deep breath, she continued, "Try not to worry about it."

The car got quiet for a second. Then a concerned and slightly confused Jenny began asking, "What are you gonna do?"

"I don't know yet," Mom answered. "But it will be fair. We need to give it some more thought first. Try not to worry."

Jenny begged, "You gotta tell me. It's not fair."

Dad piped in, "We need some time to decide on something that's fair, sweetie. Try not to worry about it so much."

As they arrived at Grandma and Grandpa's house, Mom ran into the house while Dad delayed Jenny a bit. Mom quickly explained the situation to Grandma and asked for her help. Grandma smiled and said, "I'll take care of it," and removed all of her candy bowls from sight. Have you ever noticed how grandparents often station candy bowls every two to three feet for easy grazing on holidays? Such was the way at this house—except on this particularly sad day.

As Jenny ran in, she immediately began searching for the bowls. "Where's the candy? Where's the candy? Where's the candy?"

Grandma looked at her and said sadly, "Oh! Bummer!"

"What?" cried Jenny.

"I heard what you called your mommy in the car."

"Ohhhh." Jenny mumbled.

"I give sweet candy to kids who are sweet to their parents," Grandma responded sadly.

How did Jenny respond? With all the fury of a healthy four-year-old, she hit the floor for a full-fledged temper tantrum. Grandma looked down at her and replied with enthusiasm, "Very nice fit, but I think you can do better. Why don't you practice here for a while and join us in the other room when you're done." Does Grandma know a bit of good old-fashioned Love and Logic? We think so!

❤ ❤ ❤

What Does an Appropriate Consequence Look Like?

Delaying the consequence gave Jenny's Mom and Dad plenty of time to think. That's the true benefit of this technique. What did they need to consider before taking action? Simply stated, how can we design a consequence that teaches Jenny something about the real world? How can we design a consequence that will not seem arbitrary or designed to "get even?" How can we be sure to lock in the empathy first and remain calm? How can we design a consequence that we can actually enforce?

A consequence that works best is one that "fits" the misbehavior. Spanking a child who calls her father a "butthead" is not an appropriate consequence. Why? Simply because spanking fails to teach any new skills, builds resentment, and sends the message that hitting is what you do to someone when they make you mad. I (Charles) think we've had enough of this in our society already!

An appropriate consequence is respectful to your child, as well as to you, and focuses on bad choices, not "bad" children. Consequences that work well address the present rather than past; they deal with something that's just happened recently, not something from long ago that you forgot to discuss and only recently remembered. Of course, consequences only work well when we are actually able to follow through with them. Have you ever seen a parent threaten a consequence and realize about sixty seconds later that he or she will never be able to enforce it? How sad! Lastly, consequences will only work if we can avoid lecturing, nagging, reminding, or laying a guilt trip.

Appropriate Consequences

- Fit the misbehavior.
- Focus on poor choices, not "bad" children.
- Address the present, not the past.
- Are wrapped in a loving blanket of empathy.
- Are not accompanied by lectures, reminders, or guilt trips.
- Can be enforced consistently.
- Teach your child wisdom.

Parents we meet boast about how well the delayed consequence technique works for them. They no longer have to fear not knowing what to do. They can take some time and get help from others. The best part is that there are only three steps, and they're easy to remember.

First, when you don't know what to do, delay the consequence. Lock in the empathy—"How sad," or "Bummer," or "Uh-oh"—and say, "I'm going to have to do something about this, but not now." Finally, add six magical words: "Try not to worry about it."

Second, put together a plan. Often it helps to call a friend, talk with your spouse, or get some ideas from someone else.

Third, deliver the consequences with lots of empathy. Did you notice how Grandma pulled this off with Jenny?

Three Steps in Delaying Consequences

- Say, "I'll have to do something about this, but not now. Try not to worry about it."
- Put together a plan that fits the misbehavior. Make sure the consequence is appropriate.
- Deliver the consequence with lots of empathy.

One of our favorite situations happened at a Love and Logic parenting conference. It's an example of how the delayed consequence technique turned a chaotic home into a calm one.

The first night of our Love and Logic parenting seminar, this couple had all of the typical signs of weary parents—the mother had dark circles under her eyes, and the father had an uncontrollable twitch. On the first night, they kept leaving and returning to the session . . . in and out, in and out, in and out. Finally, they gathered their things and left early.

When they returned the next evening, they looked a little more relaxed. When conference participants were asked if anyone had experimented with Love and Logic, this father stood up and smiled a happy yes.

When asked what happened, he said, "We have six-year-old twins." The audience immediately groaned their sympathy. "They've worn out almost every baby-sitter in town," he continued. "I'm sure you saw us coming and going yesterday. Well, they were acting so badly in the child care you provided that we kept getting messages to come and talk to them. Finally, they acted up so bad that the lady who's running it kicked them out. She told us they couldn't come back!

Imagine this! You are a parent. Your kids are out of control. You go to a parenting class in the hope of learning how to control them—and they get you kicked out! Feeling bad for the father, we expressed our empathy.

"Oh, it's okay," he said. "We got in the car last night and did the delayed consequence thing." You could hear the other couples' interest peak as he went on.

"When we got in the car, I looked at them in the rear-view mirror and said, "Ooooooh. This is sad. Fighting like that? We're going to have to do something about it—but not now, because we're driving. We'll come up with something really good. We'll call Grandma, Grandpa, check with the neighbors. We'll figure something out. Try not to worry."

Did this dad follow Step 1 perfectly? Absolutely!

The next day, these parents proceeded with Step 2. They called some friends and family, put together their plan, and covered all their bases.

The next night, when they put on their dress-up clothing to go back to our parenting conference, one of their twins asked, "Where are you going?"

"We're going to our parenting class," their mother said.

"Yeah," said their father. "We had a good time there."

The twins looked at each other and one of them protested. "You can't go!"

The other twin jumped in, "We got kicked out. You have to stay with us!"

At that moment, the doorbell rang. Who entered? The baby-sitter. "This is Mabel," said the twins' father. "She's going to watch you tonight."

"What?!" the twins echoed in perfect harmony.

"She charges three dollars an hour if you're sweet," said their mom, "and six dollars an hour if you're not . . ."

". . . And," their father chimed in, "she's going to ask how you plan to pay her."

"What!? Please, Dad! Don't leave us here!"

"She looks mean, Mom!"

Their parents wished Mabel a good night and walked out the door. They returned that night, after the kids were asleep. Mabel reported that the girls had behaved rather well and, she said laughing, "They kept saying, 'We don't have any money,' and they kept begging me to waive my fee!" The next morning these parents awoke to find two very concerned kids.

"We can't pay Mabel. We told her we couldn't pay her."

"No problem," their mother said to them.

"No problem at all," said their dad. "We'll pay her."

"Great!" "Cool!" said the twins.

"Then, you can pay *us* with toys."

"Oh, good!" "We can do that!" said the twins. They ran into their bedroom and came back with some of their oldest, most broken toys.

Their father applied empathy. "Oooooh, bummer!" he said. "Those toys are too broken."

The twins returned to their bedroom and came back with some small plastic toys they had received at a fast-food restaurant.

"Ooooooh, bummer!" their mother said. "Too small."

The parents were having so much fun watching their kids run back and forth, they carried the game on for a while. After several times, the twins finally returned, very slowly, with their final pick—their favorite dolls— complete with the matching pink plastic sports car.

The dad told the entire audience how powerful this method was. Next, he described the girls' responses. One just sniffled, while the other looked at him and asked, "Daddy? If you spank us, can we keep our dolls?"

❤ ❤ ❤

The twins' parents told us that they took a deep breath, trying to conceal their joy, and just said to the girls, "We used to do that, but we don't anymore."

We all applauded these parents that night—for experimenting with some new ideas, but mostly because we were happy for them. They had made a great discovery. Their empathy opened their kids' minds to learning and, by delaying the consequences, these parents were able to plan a perfect follow-up to their kids' misbehavior. And, icing on the cake, they had fun doing it.

Love and Logic Experiment #7

Have an Energy Drain

The next time your child creates a problem for you,
have an "energy drain."

The "energy drain" technique really amounts to what we call a "generic consequence." What does this mean? Simply put, parents can use this technique any time their kids create any sort of hassle for them.

Listed below are some possible reasons for having an energy drain:

- Your child lied to you about something.
- Your kids are fighting around you and it hassles your eyes and ears.
- Your child interrupts you while you are on the phone.
- Your child misbehaves at school, and you get a call from the teacher.
- Your child keeps whining and won't stop.
- Your child causes a problem for you in any other way.

The number of uses for energy drain boggles the mind!

Review "I'm Having an Energy Drain" on pages 107–108.

Notice how these two different parents applied this technique to two different problems. One used it with lying. The other used it with sibling bickering.

Ask your child how he or she plans to recharge you.

Try saying something like this, "What an energy drain. When you interrupt me on the phone, it really tires me out. How are you planning to put this energy back into me?"

When your child says something like, "I don't know," give him or her some possible options. Extra chores are a great recharging strategy.

CHAPTER EIGHT

Don't Wait until
They're Teenagers!

Good News about the Terrible Twos

Everyone has heard of "the terrible twos." It's a phrase that wreaks havoc in the hearts of parents with infants and little sweeties who are starting to crawl. They wait for their children to turn two with the same expectations as a convicted criminal awaiting a death sentence.

Two-year-olds have gotten a bad name unjustly. Sure, the second year of life is all about becoming independent and testing authority, and this can be pretty trying for parents. Are you ready for the good news?

First, experimentation with independence and testing of authority are normal and healthy signs. It's what kids at that age are supposed to do. Second, Love and Logic offers some really practical tools for making this age more fun for parents. That's right—fun! Third, the lessons learned at this age pave the way for how children will deal with authority figures for the rest of their lives. In other words, the lessons we teach our kids at an early age tend to stick.

That's why Love and Logic parents don't wait fourteen years. They start when their kids are young enough to carry, so they can enjoy teen years with kids who are respectful, responsible, and fun to be around.

The best predictor of an out-of-control teenager
is a two-year-old who runs the house.

Good News for Parents of Two-Year-Olds

- Your child's desire to be independent and to test authority
  is normal and healthy.
- Practical Love and Logic tools can make this age more fun
  for parents.
- If you parent really well during the first three years of life,
  chances are that your child will become a responsible
  teenager who is fun to be around.

Becoming a Loving Authority Figure

Children thrive when they view their parents as loving and a
bit strict at the very same time. This is what we mean when we
say "loving authority figure." When children lack such adults in
their lives they often feel out of control and act that way. Their
self-esteem suffers, and they tend to spend their lives making poor
decisions. Luckily, it's never too early to establish yourself as a
loving authority figure in your child's life. How? Everything we've
talked about so far has been devoted to helping you achieve this
goal. The four principles of Love and Logic, the two basic rules,
and what we've learned about needs and wants—all of it helps
parents and other care providers achieve this all important goal.

Handle Them without Breaking a Sweat

We've said it before. The first step is showing your kids that
you can handle them without breaking a sweat. In other words,

show them that you can handle their misbehavior without anger and frustration, and without threats and repeated warnings.

One of our favorite examples is what happened with little Arturo. Have you ever noticed how two-year-olds tend to pick restaurants as the best places for all-out free-for-alls? Because this had become somewhat of a chronic problem with little Artie, his mother and father decided to try a bit of Love and Logic. After spending some time planning, Mom and Dad decided to have an "Authority Figure Training Session" (AFTS) at a local restaurant.

Wise parents plan ahead. They predict when their kids will have fits and put a plan together before they go. Then, they can actually look forward to their children misbehaving. The reason? The road to wisdom is paved with mistakes. Here's what transpired with Arturo.

When he and his family went out to eat, little Artie refused to sit in his high chair, and started to whine, "I hate this place! I hate this place! No!"

His father looked at him with sadness in his eyes and asked softly, "Is this a wise decision, Art?" Arturo continued his fit.

Arturo's mom piped up sweetly, "How sad. Looks like Artie needs to go and sit in the back room until he understands how to behave when he's eating with us." Earlier in the week, these Love and Logic parents had phoned a number of restaurants until they'd found one whose manager agreed to help them out with a little "thinking area" for Arturo. (By the way, some parents simply use the rest room as the "thinking area.")

Artie began to wail as his father carried him back to the coat room of the restaurant. Luckily, Artie's dad knows a neat trick for handling wailing and other such frustrating behavior.

One way to stop irritating behaviors is to encourage them.

Encourage an obnoxious behavior? Why? When we encourage a child to do something he's going to do anyway, we remain in charge. We avoid a power struggle. Encouraging the behavior also causes many children to reason, "My parents actually want me to throw this fit! I'll show them. I'll stop. Nobody can make me throw a fit if I don't want to."

Arturo's father looked into his eyes and calmly said, "The really good thing about this room is that it's okay to cry and yell back here. Sometimes it's just best to scream it out. I think it would be good if you just yelled as loud as you can."

Artie glared back at his father, "No! I don't want to yell!"

Dad responded, "Ok, but I think it might help."

Art sat for about two seconds then stood up and began to stomp loudly. His father said softly, "Make sure you do some good stomping if you're going to stomp. The last time you stomped it was really kind of boring. I'll wait right outside until you are ready to act nice. Then you can come out."

❤ ❤ ❤

Children cannot achieve true autonomy without first learning how to respond properly to authority.

Kids cannot become truly responsible, happy, and independent until they've learned how to deal with authority in an appropriate way. Real freedom cannot be attained without accepting and sharing respect and responsibility.

Age two, Arturo's father learned, is all about teaching kids how to take "no" for an answer. He also learned some Love and Logic magic to make this happen. Since he and his wife had locked in the "Uh-oh" song at home first, Artie only had to spend a few minutes in the back room.

Wise parents know that the first step toward getting their toddlers to behave in public is getting them to behave at home.

A much cuter and sweeter Arturo walked back to the table with his dad. What did his parents say when he returned? They didn't lecture, threaten, or rub salt into the wounds. Instead, they said enthusiastically, "Good to have you back, Sweetie! We love you." They resisted the urge to say something like, "I hope you learned your lesson, young man." They know that the consequence is the lesson and that their son is smart enough to learn from it.

A while ago, we met a single mother with two little boys and one little girl. She used a different strategy for dealing with restaurant rampages. Susie was having a very bad evening, so bad that she began spreading mashed potatoes in her hair and wailing, "Yucky 'tatoes! Yucky 'tatoes."

Mom picked up her cell phone, dialed a number, and said, "It's time!" Ten minutes later, her friend arrived at the restaurant, carried Susie to the car, and took her home. When Mom walked in the door with the boys, she made sure that each was eating an ice cream cone.

Little Susie wailed, "Ice cream! They got ice cream? Not fair!"

Mom turned to her and said softly, "What a bummer. This is so sad. I give ice cream to children who act sweet when we're in a restaurant. By the way, which toy are you going to use to pay for your baby-sitting?"

❤ ❤ ❤

Do you think Susie is beginning to see her mommy in a new light? Is Mom establishing herself as a loving authority figure? Are you guessing Susie will be quite a bit sweeter the next time they eat out?

More Thoughts on What We Mean by "Loving Authority Figure"

As we now know, there's one cardinal rule for the first few months of a child's life: Do everything to meet your infant's basic needs! Snuggle, make lots of eye contact, smile, and take away any physical pain or discomfort. When an infant cries, we *do not* leave him or her alone in his room or crib. Instead, we meet the needs that are causing the crying.

While loving parental authority figures want their children to be happy, and they meet their children's basic needs as consistently as possible, they don't become "doormats." They don't respond to "wants" in the same way they respond to needs. If they did, they'd be run ragged by a demanding and obnoxious toddler. They know that the first rule of parenting is to take good care of yourself. They also realize how important it is that they teach their children the difference between needs and wants.

People almost universally remark that "strict, but loving" parents, teachers, coaches, religious leaders, and other adults were the people who had the greatest positive influence on them when they were kids.

Love and Logic believes in this combination and teaches us how to become the most loving people in our children's lives while at the same time being some of the strictest.

What Love and Logic Authority Figures Give Kids

- Unconditional love and respect
- High expectations and firm limits
- Some freedom within those limits
- Time and encouragement to struggle through difficult challenges
- Guidance in solving problems within those challenges
- An understanding of the difference between needs and "wants"
- Positive, self-confident role models

True Authority Figures Are Both Powerful and Kind

Truly successful authority figures don't have a long list of rules to be followed. They command respect, because they offer it. They set limits, because they understand that we all need them.

They give children choices, because they know that decision-making prepares a child for a world filled with important, potentially life-and-death choices. As a result, a child who is fed a diet of Love and Logic develops an enhanced self-concept, a feeling of self-respect—one that says, "Yes! I can do it!" "Yes! I'm capable!"

**Wise parents begin the process
of becoming loving authority figures
during the first days of their child's life.**

Through eye contact, smiles, hugs, and meeting basic needs, parents lay a foundation of love. As "wants" begin to emerge for their child, they begin to set very firm, yet kind, limits. They realize that the best way to have fun with their teenagers is to be strong and loving with their toddlers! Kids learn some of their first lessons about loving authority while playing with their parents.

Four-year-old Ralph loves to wrestle with his dad and play roughly. His father roughhouses with Ralph, because he knows his child enjoys it, but he's careful to make sure that nobody gets hurt. Ralph pushes against his father, who pushes back with the same gentle intensity, holding Ralph in place. Then he quickly lets go, surprising little Ralphie a bit.

"More! More!" Ralph yells, giggling, when his father lets go. Then Ralph's dad holds him gently, and Ralph shouts, "Let me go! Let me go!"

His father lets go. Then, in a surprise attack, he gently jumps on top of Ralph, until Ralph squeals with delight, "Get off me!" His dad holds on a few seconds longer, then lets go. They both have a great time.

❤ ❤ ❤

Roughhousing may be more common with little boys than little girls, but it's good for girls, too! What can kids learn from this kind of play? They learn that their parents love them, sometimes give them some control, and that their parents are strong. The result of roughhousing is that kids develop an image of their parents as people who are powerful and kind at the same time.

What Kids Learn from Gentle Roughhousing

- Their parents love them.
- Their parents are strong people and can control them.
- Their parents won't control them unless it's necessary.
- Parents are people who are powerful, kind, and gentle at the same time.
- They love their parents and want to be like them.

A little roughhousing helps kids bond with their parents and teaches them about authority. If you've ever had the opportunity to watch documentaries about how wolves live in the wild, you know that they have a rather complex social order. The way they learn to live with the pack and be productive members of their community is to wrestle with their parents when they're cubs.

Once in a while, the father or mother wolf will put a large paw right on top of the little cub and growl a little. The little cub will look up and think, "Uh-oh!" and then the parent will let the cub up quickly. No one gets hurt, but the young wolves begin to understand that they can have fun and declare their independence, but there are obviously other beings who are in charge! Do you think there's a lot we can learn from the animal kingdom?

Play and Discipline: Two Parts of a Whole

In most mammal families, roughhousing between parents and kids goes on all the time. True authority figures know that love and respect are counterparts, that parents need to create a balance between play and discipline. Some parents try too hard to assume complete control over a child, which never allows them to fully establish themselves as authority figures.

True authority figures consider the following question on a daily basis: "How would I want my child to treat me if the roles were reversed?" Certainly, these roles may indeed be reversed someday. Think of it this way: How do you want to treat someone who may someday be choosing your nursing home?

Love and Logic parents give as much freedom or control as possible in areas in which they don't need it.

No authority figure can maintain control by power alone. The great leaders in history have always known that their power relied on their ability to do two things: set limits, and get people to fall in love with them.

Kids Don't Come with Instruction Manuals

Sadly, some parents never successfully establish themselves as loving authority figures. Some believe love means being either overly protective, or overpowering and threatening. Since kids don't come with instruction manuals, we all just do our best. Often we realize that our own parents seem to sit on our shoulders, so to speak, and tell us how to act with our kids. In other words, how we were treated as children . . . our own parents' voices and actions . . . become "tapes" in our subconscious minds, directing how we act toward our own children.

Parents Who Are Dictators

Sometimes we are raised with tapes in our minds that guide us to "bark" orders rather than set limits in a loving way. At the Love and Logic Institute, we refer to these parents as "Drill Sergeants." If their children do not follow their commands with precision, these parents wield lectures, threats, and punishments in an attempt to assert control. Isn't it ironic that parents who attempt to hoard control wind up losing most of it?

The environment such parents create is really a dictatorship. Under dictatorial rule, people do not learn to make decisions. Rather, they learn to do what they're told only to avoid punishment or earn rewards. Children raised by Drill Sergeants do not learn how to think for themselves, because they never have to think! When children are reprimanded or punished for "being bad," the only emotions they feel are fear and resentment—feelings that prevent them from focusing on the choices they've made and how to make better ones in the future.

We typically see one or two different types of teens created by Drill Sergeant parents. Some teens openly rebel or sneak around behind their parents' backs. These teenagers make lots of poor choices, just to show their parents who's boss. Other teens with Drill Sergeant parents never learn to think for themselves. Faced with peer pressure, they make faulty decisions because they haven't had practice.

"Drill Sergeant" Parents

- Bark orders that they demand be followed.
- Use punishment to assert their control.
- Encourage kids to never learn how to think for themselves.
- Inspire fear and resentment rather than problem-solving.
- Create teenagers who can't think for themselves.

The following family story is a sobering example of what can happen to kids brought up by Drill Sergeant parents. Not all of our stories have such tragic results, but we were moved by this story and believe it makes a memorable point.

A father we met at a conference felt embarrassed in front of teachers and other parents, because he said he'd made a lot of mistakes. He said he'd grown up in a family where everyone was bossed around by a father who barked a lot of orders that everyone was expected to follow.

Never having learned anything different, he accepted this way of life as the only way. Since he believed it had worked when he was a child, he started to use it with his own kids. Now he was coming to a Love and Logic conference with hopes of encouraging other parents not to make the same mistake.

A Tale of Two Teens

Joseph had two children who were as different as day and night. When the first child was born, one of the nurses in the maternity ward looked at this baby girl and said, "Oh, what a sweet child! Wish I could take her home."

"The nurses were right," Joseph told us. "From that time on, Jesse always tried to figure out what we wanted, so she could please us. We told her what to do, and she did it.

"Our second little child came along," Joseph said. "The maternity ward nurses looked at this baby and didn't say a thing. They were probably thinking, 'What a sweet little girl. Sure glad she's not ours!'

Maternity nurses often have an uncanny ability to see into a child's personality. Why? Because they have worked with thousands of newborns. This infant turned out to be a real challenge. She wouldn't eat when she was supposed to eat, she cried more often, and she soon became a very rebellious child.

"As she grew up," Joseph told us, "she tried to find out exactly what we wanted, so she could do the opposite. It's amazing," he said, sadly, "that we raised them just about the same, and they turned out so different."

"Jesse, the older one, would come to breakfast wearing a mini-skirt and I'd tell her to go right back upstairs and change into something more appropriate for school. She would smile

College of the Ouachitas

sweetly and say okay. Then she'd come down wearing something akin to a prairie dress from the old frontier days. Like I said, she liked to please us.

Jacqueline, the youngest, would come down in a miniskirt, I'd tell her to change, and she'd come back downstairs in a long skirt. One day, her mother discovered that she was folding her mini-skirt up and throwing it in her backpack. When she got to school, she'd change back into the skirt she'd wanted to wear.

"Jesse always did what she was asked," Joseph told us, "and Jackie always fought back. Brought them up the same," he repeated. Then he got very quiet and told us the rest.

"The girls took the keys to the car one night, without permission, to participate in drag racing with some other kids. That was the last time I ever saw them alive. They both died in a car crash. I'm here today, not to collect your sympathy, but because I don't want you to lose your kids the way I lost mine. I didn't realize, until it was too late, that I lost my kids by bossing them around.

"Jackie was strong-willed, and it's obvious that I lost her by bossing her around. She rebelled by making bad decisions, just to prove that she could have her own way. But I lost Jesse by bossing, too. When her sister invited her to go drag racing, she didn't know enough to say, 'I better not. This is not a wise decision.' We never taught her to think for herself. We just told her what to do and how to do it. We turned her into a perfect target for some of her rebellious peers. If it hadn't been her sister, it might have been someone else."

❤ ❤ ❤

As much as we don't like to hear what happened to Joseph, at the Love and Logic Institute we tell this story. Why? Because it helps parents understand the potential danger in trying to maintain complete control over their children.

Parents Who Search and Rescue

At the other end of the spectrum are parents who try to make their kids happy all the time. They act like helicopters. What's the job of a helicopter? To perform search and rescue missions. Parents who take this approach hover over their kids and rescue them from the consequences of poor decisions or misbehavior. What's the unfortunate result? They raise children who soon believe that the world revolves around them and that they should never be held accountable.

Sitting at the dinner table, Eric is served some eggs by his mother. Upon seeing them, he says, "Yuck! I don't want that! No!"

His mom says, "Honey, I made them for you. You need to eat your eggs."

"No!" the boy insists. "I'm not eating them! I hate them!"

"Oh, Honey," his mother says, "All right. What do you want?"

"I want Pop Tarts!" the child demands.

"Okay, Sweetie," his mother says. "I'll make you Pop Tarts this time, but not again. Drink your orange juice."

"I don't want orange juice," the boy says angrily. "I don't *want* it! I want soda!"

"Honey, soda isn't for breakfast. That's not what we have..."

"I want soda!" he yells.

"Okay, just this time. But only this time, okay?"

❤ ❤ ❤

This mother, trying to be a good mom, provided cafeteria service for Eric. Whenever he refused to eat what he was served, he got what he requested. Trying to be strict on occasion, Eric's mom would say, "No. You're eating that. I'm not getting you anything else." Eric would refuse to eat and wait it out.

Two hours later, after not eating, he'd come to his mother and whine, "I'm hungry." Guess what would happen? She would invariably rush to get him some food. Instead of being wise enough to say, "How sad," this mother gave her child everything he requested.

When Eric turned seven, he got into the habit of forgetting his lunch. He would call his mother, and she would rush to school. Each time she'd bring two sack lunches instead of one. Why two? Just in case he lost another one of them before lunch!

When he was twelve, Eric's teacher assigned a science project. He complained to his mother, "But this is really hard. Not fair."

"Don't worry. I'll take care of it." Then she completed it for him. What was the the good news? Mom earned an "A."

When Eric was seventeen, Mom hired the best lawyer in town to get him out of some hot water; and when he was twenty-three, Eric got caught stealing some antique jewelry his mother had inherited from her grandmother.

❤ ❤ ❤

Isn't that ironic? You treat kids well—you do everything for them—and they end up treating *you* badly! Why? Because when we continually rescue our kids, they become dependent on us, which eventually fills them with resentment. This syndrome is called "hostile dependency." When kids are forced to be dependent on someone, they become resentful, because down deep, every human being yearns to be free, competent, and independent. Down deep, Eric knows his mother crippled him. Now he hates her for it.

The more we rescue our kids from everything they encounter, the more they end up hating us in the long run.

When Eric's mother asked, "How could you do that—steal jewelry—after all we've done for you?" Eric said, "You never did anything for me. You never cared."

The good news is that its never too late to change. Yes! An old dog can learn new tricks. Why are we so sure about this? Because of the many parents we've met who've changed their ways. I (Charles) received a letter from a father who saw himself as a "recovering helicopter dad." In his letter, he described how he used to park his car across the street from his son's school, sit there, and focus his binoculars on the playground. When his child went out for recess, he'd keep watch just to make sure that nothing bad happened! After learning Love and Logic, Dad realized how he was crippling his son. Now he allows his son to learn from the occasional playground disputes that every child encounters. Yes! It's never too late to change.

"Helicopter" Parents

- Continually hover over and "save" their children.
- Try too hard to make their children's lives "perfect."
- Create feelings of "hostile dependency" in their kids.
- Bring up children who don't know how to be responsible.
- Cause kids to feel unhappy and incapable.

Both Drill Sergeant and Helicopter parents love their kids and do what they do because they believe it's right. Unfortunately, none of these parents ever establish themselves as loving authority figures. Neither the Drill Sergeant nor the Helicopter parent is able to be strict and loving at the same time. Neither prepares their children to make wise choices in a sometimes confusing and dangerous world.

Unintentionally, both say to their kids, "Sweetie, you are so incapable that I have to think for you. I have to constantly save you from yourself." Is it surprising, then, that both types of parents raise resentful kids with poor self-concepts?

Why We Parent the Way We Do

Parents almost always do the best they can. Most parents love their kids more than anything else in their lives. Still, in today's world, it's tougher than ever to raise responsible children.

How Do We Choose Our Parenting Style?

Our own experiences as kids have a great impact on how we parent. Our tendency is to go one of two ways. Some of us believe that the parenting we got was great—made us who we are today. As a result, we make the decision to parent as we were parented. Sometimes we are aware of this decision on a conscious level. Even more frequently, we've made this choice on deeper subconscious level.

In contrast, some of us believe that our parents could have done a lot better, or were incapable of parenting well, or just plain blew it. What decision do we make then? Looking back at our own childhood, we tend to parent in the opposite fashion. Again, this decision is most frequently made on the subconscious level.

Let's take a look at some of the choices we've seen parents make over the years.

• **"I don't want my kids to have to struggle like I did."** Anita grew up in a loving home, but money was always tight. The family used crates for chairs, started a garden and raised chickens for food. She grew up feeling that she would make things different for her own kids. She struggled and eventually developed a very successful business. With her own children, she spends most of her time giving them everything they want and keeping them happy. She can't understand why they're so demanding and ungrateful.

• **"I hate my parents for what they did to me."** Rod grew up with parents who yelled and screamed. Never knowing when he might be ridiculed or hit, he had a painful childhood. When he looked down at his newborn daughter, Emily, he whispered to her, "You will never feel the pain I did!" Like Anita, he spends his life protecting his child from the world.

• **"It worked for me!"** Thelma grew up in a traditional family, in a small town, at a time when the world was a lot simpler. She grew up feeling that her stern parents had done her a great favor by using angry lectures, threats, and spankings. Back then, children rarely considered disobeying their parents. Today, she's finding that anger and frustration don't work. She now spends most of her time feeling angry because her kids are sneaking around behind her back. The other day, her teenager cracked a smile as she was lecturing him about respect.

• **"My parents were Love and Logic parents, and they didn't even know it!"** Jerry always wished his parents would yell at him or spank him. Instead, they expected him to solve his own problems and provided empathy before delivering consequences. He realizes now that they were strict, but very loving at the same time. Jerry grew up not thinking much about how he was raised. All he knows is that parenting is almost automatic for him. For someone like Jerry, it's easy to avoid becoming a Helicopter or Drill Sergeant.

Most parents want to raise great kids and have the best of intentions. Few people have the goal of raising irresponsible, nasty kids. Instead, almost everyone sets out to teach their children responsibility and show them love. How they choose to do it, however, can sure make a difference in how things turn out. Parents who want to make some changes can! We've seen it over and over again. How do they do it? They go slow by picking just one Love and Logic technique, experimenting with it, and seeing how it works. When they see some success, they move on and try another. That's why we have included the LOVE AND LOGIC EXPERIMENTS at the end of each chapter. These are great ways to get your feet wet. Take it slow, be patient with yourself, and have fun.

Caution!
Wise parents don't try every single Love and Logic technique at once. Instead, they take it slow and experiment with one or two simple ideas at a time and have some fun.

There are no guarantees in life—no absolutely certain approaches to ensure that our children grow up to be lovable, kind, intelligent, reliable people. The odds are raised, however, when we start young and follow the two rules of Love and Logic. Let's review for a moment.

LOVE AND LOGIC RULE #1 FOR PARENTS:

Take care of yourself by setting limits in a loving way.

- Act without frustration or anger.
- Stop using threats and repeated warnings.
- Set a limit once.
- Make statements you can enforce.
- Give kids a healthy sense of control.

LOVE AND LOGIC RULE #2 FOR PARENTS:

Turn every mistake or misbehavior into a learning opportunity.

- Always provide a strong dose of empathy *before* delivering a consequence.
- Replace punishment with logical consequences.
- When possible, show your child how to solve his or her own problem.

You don't have to be a perfect parent to raise a great kid!

Love and Logic Experiment #8

"Uh oh. Looks like a little bedroom time."

Review Steps for the "Uh-oh" Song on pages 74–75.

Give yourself plenty of planning time before trying this technique.

For at least two weeks, follow these steps exactly.

Remember: The best ways to sabotage this technique are to get frustrated and angry or to use too many words. Allow the consequence to do the teaching.

What should you do if your child cries and throws a major fit in the room?

The Uh-oh Song is often harder for the parent than for the child. When he or she is throwing a fit in the room, say to yourself,

"Sometimes we have to make our kids really upset in the short term so they can be happy and responsible in the long term."

Remember to have lots of fun with your kids when they are behaving well.

The Uh-oh Song will not work unless the child loves to be with you so much that he or she misses you when alone in the room.

After two weeks notice how your child responds to the words "Uh-oh!"

Parents all over the country tell us that their kids—as a result of this technique—learn to listen the first time, don't misbehave as much, and are a whole lot happier.

CHAPTER NINE

Potholes along the Road to Responsibility

It Can Be a Bumpy Road

Every journey has its obstacles, and every parent encounters problems with their children as they grow. Some of these problems are very small, whereas others are quite large and troubling. No matter how hard we have worked to smooth the way and to avoid the parental hazards, it's inevitable that we'll hit an occasional "pothole" along the way.

Some parents get stuck and sink forever into negative patterns with their children. Others fall into the very same holes yet quickly climb their way out. When we've fallen in, it can be very dark and hard to see. Some parents refuse to admit to themselves or others that they've made some mistakes or that their young children are beginning to have problems. Others feel their way through the darkness, forgive themselves for their mistakes, take healthy action, and see their children blossom.

It can be very hard to admit when our children begin to fall into negative patterns. It can be even harder to admit that we're making some parenting mistakes. Be kind to yourself! Everyone makes them. We love our kids so much that we don't want to believe it when things aren't working. We all have dreams for how our children will turn out—they'll be happy, successful, have lots of friends, get married, and provide us with wonderful grandchildren. Is it really scary when these dreams are threatened? Sure! What's the good news? First, nobody is asking you to be perfect. Imperfect parents have been known to raise wonderfully responsible and happy kids. Secondly, when we're brave enough to look at our mistakes, there are plenty of solutions to be found.

Common Potholes

Parents are biologically programmed to protect their young. Part of our "wiring," this programming drives us to meet their basic needs and shield them from harm. This, obviously, is a very good thing! Looking at the other side of the coin, this drive may also make it harder for us to admit that our children are beginning to learn some unhealthy habits. Clearly, it is human nature to make excuses for our children. We do this out of love. Sadly, some parents allow excuses to get in the way of making some changes that really need to happen early in a child's life. The real tragedy is that behavior and personality problems get harder to correct with each year of a child's life. Young children are very flexible. They typically snap out of bad behavior very quickly. I (Charles) have provided therapy to many families of older children and teens. What did I learn? Stated very simply, wise parents take simple actions early on so they can avoid having to take major, painful ones later in the child's life.

Wise parents take simple actions early on so they can avoid having to take very painful ones later.

The following are some common traps, or "potholes" that many parents of young kids fall into. The first step is recognizing that anyone can fall into them. The second step is forgiving yourself if you have. The third step is experimenting with some Love and Logic solutions.

TRAP #1: *"He's Just Going through a Phase"*

Little William is an energetic toddler who loves going to the grocery store with Mom. Why? Because he has more fun there than at the circus. He runs up and down the aisles, begs for candy, and revs his little engine while Mom goes bananas. "William? Get over here! Leave that alone. Don't go over there. If you grab that jar, you're not gonna get any candy. Wait 'til I tell your dad!" William is greatly entertained by his mother's exasperation, and he loves the attention he gets when she shouts.

In his travels throughout the store, William finds an unsuspecting victim. A grandfatherly gentleman is doing some shopping in the candy aisle. Soon, William is turning on the charm and begging *him* for a lollypop.

William's mother is searching for him. As she rounds the corner, and sees what is happening, she screams, "William! Get over here! Leave that man alone! Finally she grabs him by the arm, pulls him away, and says to the gentleman, "I'm so sorry. You know, he's going through one of those phases these days. He just won't listen to anything I say."

We're all concerned about William! What troubles us the most is the possibility that his mother might be saying the very same thing in ten or twelve years: "I'm so sorry officer. He's going through one of those phases these days. You know how teenagers are. He just won't listen to anything I say."

William's mom may not recall, when she looks back on her son's life, that this "phase" started as soon as he was able to hear her say "no." Children who are not taught early on to take "no" for an answer are the ones who don't know how to "just say no" to drugs, alcohol, and violence as teenagers. By the time they reach their preteen or teen years, it is really too late to teach this lesson. When your toddler is "going through a phase" the *only* time to do something about it is right now.

What might William's mom try? First, we'd ask her to practice the "Uh-oh" Song at home. Remember: children are more likely to behave in public if this is locked in first at home. Secondly, we'd probably ask her to find a grocery store where the shopping carts have seat belts. Thirdly, we'd suggest that she respond in this way as soon as William becomes wild: "Uh-oh," Looks like a little cart time. This is so sad." Then we'd recommend her picking him up, putting him in the cart, strapping him in, and saying to herself, "I didn't come to the store today to build a long-term relationship with these other shoppers. If I can keep my mouth shut and stay firm, life is going to get a lot better for everyone involved." If Mom can take these steps, will both of their lives be better when he's fifteen? Absolutely! By the way, we know one mother who placed her child's car seat in the shopping cart. As soon as little Bertie started to bellow in the store, Mom would sing, "Uh oh. Looks like a little car seat time." It didn't take long before she got to leave the car seat in the car and enjoy a sweeter acting Bertie in the store.

TRAP #2: *"Since we're together so much, she doesn't listen to a thing I say."*

Cindy's teacher called Mom and asked her to come in for a parent–teacher conference. Since many teachers these days also invite the child, Cindy came along too. While her mommy and her teacher sat in tiny plastic chairs and visited, Cindy began noisily running around the room.

Her teacher looked over at her and said, "Cindy, please come over here and sit with us." Cindy walked right over and sat down. After about five minutes, Cindy became bored, got up, and once again began running around the room.

This time it was Mom's turn. "Cindy, come over here, okay?"

Cindy kept running. Turning to the teacher, Mom lamented, "We're together so much that she just won't listen to a word I say."

How would we respond if a preschool teacher argued, "I'm with these kids all day, so they just won't listen?" Probably just slightly better than a spouse who announces one evening, "Dear,

I'm with you so much that I just can't seem to listen or behave well for you. I just can't help it. You understand, don't you?"

All humor aside, don't fall into the trap of believing that spending a lot of time with your kids causes them to become "immune" to your discipline. Listed below are some experiments Cindy's mom might try:

Love and Logic Experiments for Cindy's Mom

1. **Use the "Uh oh" Song.** Cindy's mom might have sang, "Uh oh. Looks like a little time in the thinking chair." Or, "Uh oh, looks like time for you to sit in the hall so I can talk with your teacher."

2. **Have an "energy drain."** Mom might have delayed the consequence until that evening and said, "What a bummer. I was thinking of taking you to Silly Pete's Pizza, but after all of your running around while I was talking with your teacher, I don't have the energy."

3. **Try the "baby-sitter" routine.** "What a bummer," Mom says, "the conference was such hard work for me—I had to keep asking you not to run around—that I'm all worn out and need some relaxing time. Your dad and I are going out on a relaxation date tonight. How are you planning to pay your baby-sitter?"

TRAP #3: *"Other people let him do whatever he wants."*

Love and Logic parents believe that kids are smart enough to adapt to the different discipline styles of the adults they know. Children quickly learn to behave well for people who set and enforce solid, loving limits—and very poorly for those who don't. Love and Logic parents also believe that it's a waste of valuable time and energy to blame other adults for their own children's misbehavior.

What's a parent to do if Grandma or Aunt Lucy or a divorced spouse does a lousy job of discipline while the kids are in their presence? As hard as it is to admit, the only thing we can actually control is how *we* behave—not how Grandma or Lucy or a divorced spouse does. Wise parents in this position grit their teeth, avoid blaming other adults in front of their kids, and spend most of their energy focusing on how they—themselves—can do the best parenting possible. In contrast, unwise parents spend most of their time and energy trying to control the uncontrollable—how other adults act around their kids. These parents soon find it impossible to stay positive and often begin to model lots of frustration, anger, and hopelessness in front of their kids.

> Brian had just returned from a weekend at his father's house. Sitting at the dining room table with his mother, he started burping with great gusto.
> Mom, shocked by the display, reacted, "You stop that! That's bad manners. Cut it out right now!"
> Brian burped again, because he immediately noticed how he could use this behavior to control his mommy. "Wow," he realized down deep, "look how red her face is getting. What fun!"
> "You stop that, young man!" Mom continued to lecture.
> Looking into her eyes, Brian grinned a bit and said, "But Dad lets me."

Why is Brian misbehaving? Is it because his father allows him to burp at the table? Not really. In the best of all worlds, Daddy would do a better job of setting limits over this issue, but do you suppose that Brian can learn to behave better for his mother than for his father? Absolutely!

The true reason for Brian's belching bonanza is his mother's reaction. Remember, anger and frustration feed misbehavior. The best way to make a nasty habit stick is by getting visibly upset and frustrated about it in front of your kids. How can Mom teach Brian to save his gastric expressions for Dad's dinner table? Let's take a look at some Love and Logic experiments.

Love and Logic Anti-Belching Experiments

1. **"What a bummer. Dinner's Over."** Mom might use an enforceable statement like, "I serve dinner to kids with good manners at the table. As soon as Brian belches—the very first time he does it—she takes his plate and says, "What a bummer. Dinner's over." Then she keeps her mouth shut and lets the empathy and consequence do the teaching.

2. **Encourage the behavior in another location.** She picks Brian up, puts him in his room and says, "Here's a place where you can burp all you want. Burp as loud as you can in here. You can make your burps a lot better than you've been making them lately. Stay here and practice. Burp them all out. Come out as soon as they're gone."

When Brian comes out, his mother sees that there's still a devilish look in his eyes. Smiling at him, she says, "Go back in there and burp some more. I can tell by the way your tummy is sticking out that you've got more in there. Come out when they are all gone." By the time Brian comes out, he's pretty exhausted from all of this practice. As a matter of fact, he's ready for a nap!

3. **Have a disgust-induced "energy drain."** "Oh Brian," Mom says, "your burping drained the energy right out of me. How sad. Which of my chores are you going to do to recharge me?"

TRAP #4: *"What can you expect? She's only three."*

Some parents use age to excuse their children's misbehavior. "He's just so little. Give him a break." Love and Logic parents know that young children can learn. They know that young children can remember. Most importantly, they know that young children can learn and remember how to act nasty *or* learn and remember how to act nice. The choice is ours to make.

Olympia, who works at home, was in the middle of an important phone call. Sadly, her three-year-old kept interrupting her. "Mom! I need a drink of water! I want my puzzles. I can't reach them! Mom! Blow up this balloon! Mom! Mooommm!"

Olympia, says into the phone, "I'm sorry. Can you repeat yourself? I didn't hear what you said." As the phone call continues, she keeps getting distracted by her daughter and having to ask the other person to repeat herself.

The woman on the other end of the line, hearing the entire commotion and getting quite irritated, asks, "Can you ask your child to stop for a moment so we can finish this call?" Rather insulted, Olympia replies, "She's just a little child. What do you expect?"

Some Love and Logic experiments for Olympia.

1. The "Uh oh" Song. After the very first interruption, Mom might offer to call the person back, end the phone call, and sing, "Uh oh, looks like a little bedroom time. You can come out as soon as you are calm and I've finished this call."

2. Have an energy drain. "How sad. All of these interruptions really tired me out while I was on the phone. Now I'm too tired to take you too the pool."

3. Use the "Long, Long Phone Call" technique. Olympia might call a friend and say, "I need to talk with you for a long, long time." The more her daughter interrupts her while she is on the phone, the longer the phone call gets. She tells her daughter, "How sad. The more you interrupt me, the longer this is going to take."

Olympia might even stay on the phone after her friend hangs up! As soon as her child is quiet for two or three minutes, she hangs up and says, "When you're quiet it helps me finish my call. Thank you. I can get off the phone so much faster when you get quiet. I love you."

It doesn't take many long phone calls for a child to learn that it's smartest to leave Mom and Dad alone while they're talking!

TRAP #5: *"Sure she's a handful, but she's so creative—so intelligent!"*

Little Sara, along with lots of other kids, is enjoying a romp in the neighborhood swimming pool. Parents are watching as their kids have a great time. Sara starts teasing other kids, splashing them, taking their toys, pushing them off of their rafts, calling names, being bossy, and acting downright nasty. "This is my raft!" She complains to one child. "Nanny nanny boo boo. I got your ball. You can't get me," she teases another. "You're too slow you big dummy," she says to another. How long is it going to take before Sara has no friends? How long will it be before every kid in the neighborhood starts to avoid her like the plague?

Watching with another parent, Sara's dad smiles and says, "She can really be a challenge, but she's so intelligent and creative. I just don't think that other kids can understand her. She's so bright. She's just on another level."

It's difficult to understand why some of us fall into this trap with our kids. Perhaps because it's a whole lot easier to see our children as creative and misunderstood than obnoxious and irritating? Perhaps it also has something to do with the "tortured artist" stereotype? For some reason, our society has come to associate creativity with irresponsibility. Where did this begin? It seems that all one has to do, if one wants to get away with being rude or nasty, is to claim genius or say, "I'm just expressing my creative talents." What's the real truth about this? Even the most creative and intelligent people find it difficult to succeed unless they can get along with others and be responsible members of society.

A Love and Logic Solution for Sara's Dad.

Leave the fun activity. Whenever our kids misbehave at the pool, the park, a friend's house, a movie theater, or some other place they want to be, the decision is simple. Without giving repeated warnings, without lectures, and without anger and frustration, Dad needs to say something like, "Oh no. This is so sad, Sara. Looks like swimming is over for today."

I (Charles) recently went to the movie theater with my son. As the movie began, I noticed two kids throwing popcorn and creating quite a commotion. Sadly, I also noticed their mother and father giving them about fifteen warnings to stop. What's the Love and Logic parent do? As the first popcorn kernel flies, the parent says, "Please pick that up and throw it away. We will be leaving if I see you continue to misbehave." As the second kernel flies, the parent says, "What a bummer. Guess its time to go home." Then he or she follows through with actions instead of words. We do our kids a great disservice by giving them repeated warnings. Set the limit once and follow through.

Potholes along the Road to Responsibility
- "He's just going through a phase."
- "Since we're together so much, she just won't listen to me."
- "Other people let him do whatever he wants."
- "What do you expect? She's just a little child."
- "She's just so creative. Other people just can't understand."
- "I tell him and I tell him, but he just won't listen."

TRAP #6: *"I tell him and I tell him, but he just won't listen"*

When we hear parents say, "I tell him and I tell him," we're already starting to get a clue about what might be going wrong. The parent is relying on words instead of actions. Said differently, the parent has fallen into the trap of believing that more warnings, lectures, threats, or arguing will solve the problem. What do kids learn the most from? Do they learn the most from our words?

Or, instead, do they learn the most from our actions. We keep saying it: Actions speak louder than words.

Ernie is in the middle of another free-for-all with his mother at the lunch table. With a twisted little face, he demands, "I want a cookie!"

Mom replies, "You can have one after you eat your carrots."

"But why?" Ernie whines. "Dad said I don't have to."

"If you don't eat your vegetables, you're going to get sick!" Mom explains.

"Tony eats candy for lunch and he's ok." Ernie continues to argue.

This makes the veins on mom's forehead bulge. "I'm telling you no! I mean it! For crying out loud, eat those carrots or you can forget about sweets!"

Ernie mumbles, "You hate me."

Feeling a twinge of guilt, Mom replies, "How many times do I have to tell you? I love you. That's why you need to eat your carrots. There are plenty of starving kids around that would be thankful for them."

Ernie grins, "They can have them. Send 'em to them."

"That's not funny. You eat those. I paid good money for them. We don't waste food around here." And so on.

What a bummer for both Ernie and his mom! The only real solution for this one is to stop the arguing. Easier said than done? Just wait until you read the next section. Are you ready for a foolproof strategy for ending arguing and back-talk. Would you like to hear how Mom learned how to handle Ernie without breaking a sweat? If so, read on.

Arguing for Fun and Profit

Does it ever feel like kids today carry around a little manual called "Arguing for Fun and Profit"? Do you ever get tired of hearing phrases like "But why?" or "Not fair!" or "You hate me!"

or "Mom lets me!" or "If you really loved me, you would let me." Where does all of this back-talk come from anyway?

Many children learn at an early age that arguing has some payoffs. What it can win them, first of all, is an exciting show of parental frustration and anger. Many children "hook" their parents with something like "Not fair!" Then they sit back, watch, and think to themselves, "Wow! Look at me! I'm just a little kid, but I can change the color of Dad's face, the tone of Mommy's voice, maybe even the potential longevity of their cardiovascular systems!" Might this be what's happening between Ernie and his mom?

Secondly, some children learn that arguing wears their parents down and will eventually cause their parents to back down. They learn that if they nag, annoy, and pester long enough, their parents will give in.

Research on kids with major behavior problems—kids, for example, who've been in trouble with the law—shows that one of the best predictors of a child having these problems is his or her ability to pull adults into power struggles and arguments. What does this mean? Teaching your kids that arguing *does not* work is one of the most important things you will ever do!

The way we determine how a child sucks us in to a power struggle is to ask ourselves if we do any, or all, of the following:

• **Use too many threats that we can't back up.** "If you don't stop that right now, you're going to be sorry. I mean it! You stop it now! Wait 'til your dad gets home! Be nice!"

• **Try to reason with a child when he or she talks back.** "The reason you shouldn't use language like that is because I'm your parent and I'm older, and you need to respect me. Oh! Now you think this is funny! Wipe that smile off your face!"

• **Get frustrated, angry, or give in to a child's demands.** "Okay, you can have Pop Tarts, just this once, but don't you ever ask me for them again!"

Neutralizing Family Arguments

Are you ready for the fun part? Are you ready for a time-tested, proven, anti-argue approach?" Listed below are some of the Love and Logic steps that can get parents off the hook when their kids begin playing "verbal brain drain."

STEP 1: Go "brain dead," smile, and pause. Going "brain dead" means that we don't think about what the child has just said. If we do, we might unwittingly show some anger, and our child, knowing that we've been affected, will continue the misbehavior. Instead, our goal is to take a stance that shows we're in control of ourselves and can handle the child without breaking a sweat.

What does this stance look like? First, smile or look at the child with love in your eyes. Secondly, pause. Hold this pause until your child says, "What?" Children often learn very quickly—if a parent is consistent—that when Mom smiles and pauses, arguing isn't going to work.

STEP 2: Choose an empathetic "one-liner." Choose an empathetic "one-liner" from the "Love and Logic One-Liner" chart. "One-liners" can be very effective, only if they are delivered with genuine compassion and understanding.

STEP 3: Keep repeating the same "one-liner" over and over. Repeat your "one-liner" over and over again, with sadness instead of anger. "I love you too much to argue" has proven to be one of the easiest and most effective. Whispering the statement often makes this technique even more powerful.

STEP 4: If the child continues, walk away. If they follow, you may have to resort to changing their location or having a severe "energy drain." A father we knew used to say this: "What a bummer. Arguing drains energy. What are you going to do to charge me up? You can tell me tonight. Try not to worry."

Some Sample Love and Logic One-Liners

The child says:	You say softly:
"But why?"	"Why do you think?"
"I hate you" or "You hate me."	"I'm sorry you feel that way."
"Dad lets me."	"I know."
"Not fair!"	"I'll listen to you when your voice sounds like mine."
Just about anything your child might say:	"I love you too much to argue."

Remember Ernie, the child who wanted a cookie? Here's how things changed with just a little Love and Logic magic.

"Ernie," his mother says, "feel free to have a cookie after you eat your carrots."

"But why?" Ernie complains. "Dad said that I don't have to."

His mother pauses, smiles, and waits for Ernie to respond.

"What!?" Ernie whines.

His mom looks at him, smiles sweetly, and whispers, "I love you too much to argue."

"So I don't have to eat my carrots?" Ernie asks.

Still smiling, his mother says, "You can have a cookie after you eat them."

"But why?"

His mother pauses again and smiles, then waits for Ernie to respond.

"But I want the cookie now!"

Maintaining her sweetness, his mother says, "I love you too much to argue."

"You hate me!" Ernie responds.

"I love you too much to argue," his mother says.

"I want it now! I hate you!" Ernie cries.

His mother begins to sing, "Uh-oh. Looks like a little bedroom time . . ."

By now, Ernie knows what *this* means.

❤ ❤ ❤

Did you notice how this technique can make a child really angry? Why do kids get angry? Because they're not getting their way—they're losing control. Unhealthy control! One of the keys to great parenting is giving away healthy control—control within limits—while taking away unhealthy control, control that damages relationships.

**Sometimes we have to make our kids
really mad in the short term, so they can be happier
and more responsible in the long term.**

A week later, Ernie wanted to watch television. Here's what happened.

"I want to watch *Mutant Death Squad* on TV!"

"You can watch *Sesame Street* instead, Honey," his mom said.

"But why?"

Ernie's mom smiled, paused, and waited for Ernie to respond. In a moment, Ernie slumped down in a seat with his arms crossed.

"Don't say it!" he said. "I know. You love me too much to argue."

❤ ❤ ❤

Are you guessing that Ernie's mom is now a much happier woman? What's really exciting is that Ernie, overall, is now a much happier kid!

Love and Logic Experiment #9

Putting an End to Arguing

Review the steps for neutralizing arguments on page 151.

Remember: Young children who learn that arguing works for them become teenagers and adults who are really unpleasant to be around.

Review how Mom dealt with Ernie's arguing on pages 152–153.

Notice how Mom kept repeating, "I love you too much to argue."

Memorize the words, "I love you too much to argue."

Every time your child begins to argue, respond with this very same statement.

Expect this to make your child really mad.

Most children get very angry when their parents start using this technique.

Notice how much more energy you have at the end of the day.

It's amazing how fast arguing drains the energy out of us. Take good care of yourself—and your child—by putting an end to it early in his or her life.

CHAPTER TEN

The Power of Chores

Chores Build Responsibility and Self-Esteem

I (Charles) was hired by a school district to speak with teachers about classroom discipline. The evening before my presentation, a teacher picked me up at the airport. With her was her teenage son, Joe. As we walked through the airport, I couldn't help but notice what a nice kid he was. He held doors open for us and said really strange things like "please," and "thank you." As we walked by a store in the airport, he asked his mother to buy him something. She simply said, "No."

I was shocked by his response! "Okay," he said. No arguing, no back-talk, and no "attitude."

"Wait a minute!" I thought to myself, "This has got to be dream. When am I going to wake up?" I pinched myself and realized that what had just happened was actually real.

The next day, this teacher drove me back to the airport. This time her son did not come along. Seizing the opportunity, I asked, "Your son, Joe, is one of the nicest teenagers I've met in a long time. What have you done? What are you feeding that kid?"

Without reservation or hesitation, she answered, "Chores."

"What?" I asked.

Again she answered, "Chores. We started feeding him chores when he was three. That was her explanation. Giving the kid chores, since he was very little, had helped him become the nice, responsible teenager he is today. We've seen this over and over again in our work with children and their families. Kids who are expected to do meaningful chores are kids who grow up to be more responsible and more fun to be around.

Has this mother given Joe something that's missing in the lives of many kids today? Yes! When we compare children who grew up during the Great Depression with those who are growing up now, one difference is clear. Kids who grew up then had to struggle in order to survive. Times were extremely hard for most families. Kids grew up with a sense of purpose and a sense of really being needed by their families. They also grew up believing that they could accomplish almost anything if they worked hard enough. As a result, most became very responsible adults with relatively high self-concepts.

Chores teach children how to be successful

When economic times were a lot tougher, and everyone really had to pitch in, children learned early on that hard work and perseverance are just part of life. Today, many who have drug and alcohol problems are those who have never been given the gift of purpose or struggle. They have fallen into the trap of believing that good feelings come from the outside rather than the inside. These are kids who lack a sense of belonging or a sense of being needed by their families. When children don't get this feeling at home, they seek it out in other places. Some even look for it in gangs or cults.

Formula for a High Self-Concept

To achieve a strong, healthy self-concept, children have to try some things that are hard for them, struggle, be encouraged by those they love, and look back on their success. Struggling with difficult tasks, or tasks that seem too hard at first glance, is an essential part of self-concept building. How do we feel when we try something we don't believe we can do, stick with it, achieve success, and look back on our accomplishment? The answer is simple. We feel great about ourselves! A friend of ours took up mountain climbing. She was terrified by the prospect of hanging hundreds of feet above the ground by a single rope. As she struggled with her fear, enjoyed some success, and reflected on what she had done, she developed a higher level or respect for herself—and ropes!

Sadly, our society has become very confused about what makes people happy. Many of us have forgotten that happiness comes from doing great things—rather than getting great things. So, the true formula for high self-concept does not involve giving your children a lot of things that they want. It doesn't involve making them happy all of the time. It doesn't even involve telling them they are great on a daily basis. Instead, the true recipe involves giving the gift of struggle, letting them work through challenging tasks and problems, providing encouragement and unconditional love, and allowing them to take pride in their accomplishments. In short, kids feel good when they work hard and accomplish good things. Chores are an excellent way to make this happen.

Struggle + Encouragement from others + Accomplishment = Healthy Self-Concept

Getting Your Kids to Do Chores

Let's take a look at some healthy ways of giving your children the gift of struggle, through chores.

STEP 1: As soon as your child can walk, start working together.

• Play together and work together. Have fun together. Wash dishes, clean sinks, dust furniture, sweep, and so on.

- Say "please" and "thank you" so your kids are encouraged to say them, too.
- Do your best to help your child learn to associate chores with good feelings rather than bad ones.
- Do not criticize quality. Instead, focus mostly on the amount of effort your child expends. "Wow! You're really working hard!"

STEP 2: Model doing your own chores in front of your kids.

- Make sure your kids see you doing chores, working hard, struggling.
- Make sure they see how good you feel once the chores are done—your sense of completion and accomplishment.
- Think out loud as you work. Say things like, "This is hard. All right, I've got to do it. It has to get done. Okay, I'm doing it now. Wow, I'm almost finished. It's done! Boy, do I feel great now!
- It's important for children to know that we sometimes have to work hard at tasks we don't necessarily like. Lying and saying that all chores are fun, when they're really not, only creates frustration and resentment within your child later on. Be positive, but be honest.

STEP 3: Develop a "Toy Bermuda Triangle."

- When your young child leaves toys lying around and doesn't put them away, as requested, where do the toys go? To the Toy Bermuda Triangle!
- "Where are my toys?" your child asks? How do you respond? "When you pick up your toys, you get to keep them. When I pick up your toys, they go in my closet. How are you going to earn them back?"

STEP 4: Give choices about age-appropriate chores. Remember not to say "Do it now."

• Offer your child a choice in chores. Your child must choose between two chores, each of which are okay with you. "Would you like to dust the baseboards in the house, or would you like to pull weeds in the backyard?"
• Instead of always saying, "Do it now!" give away some control by allowing your child to choose between two different deadlines. "Would you like to do the chore now, or have it done by 3 p.m.? I'll show you what 3 p.m. looks like on the clock."
• Giving your child some time to complete the chore also gives you some time to plan what you will do if he or she forgets or refuses to do it! When we say, "Do it now!" we are really in a bad place if our kids say, "No!"

STEP 5: Do not pay your children for doing chores.

• Chores are a contribution to the family. Nobody gets paid for doing them.
• When your child asks, "What am I going to get for doing this?" your response is, "There's no pay for chores. Chores are part of being a family." These are everyday chores, such as doing dishes, helping with the laundry, dusting, cleaning, picking up toys, picking up toys, picking up toys!

Example: A parent can take an old sock, put it over a child's hand, spray a little polish or dusting solution on the sock, and let the child do a little dusting.

Example: A parent can ask a child to put away the silverware. Kids enjoy putting the forks where the forks go and the spoons where the spoons go—into a dishwasher or a silverware drawer.

Example: After their clothes come out of the laundry, you can show them how to fold them, and they can put them away in the proper drawer.

Example: Another good chore is cleaning the bathroom sink when a child is done using it. Parents can wet a rag and demonstrate how it's done. Parents and kids can do it together.

> **Keep in mind that when children are very young, the quality of the chore isn't as important as the effort. Also, please remember to say, "Thank you!"**

• When a child wants to earn something—money, a special activity, or a toy, a parent can say, "If you want to earn money, you can find some extra things that I would normally do. I will be happy to pay you when they are finished and done well.

STEP 6: Hope that your kids, when they're still very young, forget or refuse to do their chores.

• Do not remind your kids to do their chores. Pray that they will forget. Why? So they can learn early how to get tasks done without constant reminders or nagging.
• When a child forgets to do a chore, say to yourself, "The road to wisdom is paved with mistakes. Boy, is my child getting wise this week!"
• Do the chore for your child, or hire somebody to do it. Then, approach your child and say, "How sad. Remember when I asked you to pick up your clothes and you didn't? I love you too much to remind you. I took care of it. How are you going to pay me?"

When a child says, "I don't know," try the steps we learned in Chapter 7:

1. Lock in the empathy.
2. Say, "What are you going to do?"
3. When your child doesn't know, ask, "Would you like some ideas?"
4. Provide a menu of options:
   - "Want to hear what others have done?"
   - "Some kids decide to . . ." (fill in the blank).
   - "How would that work for you?"
5. Allow your child to choose, and learn from, the choice.

How do we prepare our kids for life, for those times when an employer asks them to do something? Do we prepare them by giving them plenty of reminders, or by teaching them to do things the first time they're asked? Give your kids a distinct advantage over most of their workforce peers. How? Teach them to do chores *without* reminders.

Something interesting happens when we worry that our children will make mistakes. When they sense our insecurity and anxiety, they usually confirm our greatest fears! On the other hand, when we look forward to their mistakes, because we know that the road to wisdom is paved with them, our kids can sense this too. What happens? When they sense our confidence, they actually tend to make smarter decisions. It's almost as if they reason, "Wow. Mom is so self-assured. She's not worried a bit. I wonder what's up her sleeve."

**Strange as it seems,
children wind up making far fewer mistakes
when we no longer fear that they will.**

Applying appropriate consequences when kids forget or refuse to do their chores is one of the most powerful Love and Logic tools. We *love* when our kids forget or refuse to do their chores at an early age—when the price tag is low. This means that by the time they're teens, or adults, these lessons will have already been learned.

The mother of that wonderfully polite and respectful teenager, Joe, told us that even though her son had never liked doing the chores he was given, when he finished she'd always notice a look of satisfaction on his face. He would never admit to liking the chores, but he always seemed proud of himself for having done the job. She also told us that even though he's now 6'5" tall, an inch taller than his father, he said to her recently, "I know that I'm taller than Dad now, but why does he still seem bigger?"

She said she just smiled at him and didn't answer, because she didn't know what to say. What is the answer? Simply stated, Joe's mother and father proved to him early on that they could be very strict yet very loving at the same time. When parents establish themselves as loving authority figures during the first three years of life, they will forever seem "big" or important in the eyes of their children—no matter how big or how old their children get.

We have had the great joy of learning a lot from all of the people we meet at our conferences. Earl was a very wise man who attended a Love and Logic conference we held in the southwest. An older gentleman, he was dressed like a cowboy. As he approached us, we noticed his friendly smile and his weathered skin. The many wrinkles in his face surely told of many a day riding horses under the blistering desert sun.

Offering a handshake, he remarked, "I've known this stuff for a long time. I do it with my horses."

I (Jim) asked, jokingly, "You mean, 'how sad' and 'what a bummer'?"

"No! Not that part," he smiled. "When they're still small, I show 'em that I can be kind and real strong at the same time. When they're still real small, I get down and play with 'em, wrestle with 'em and move 'em around. They grow to love me, but they also know I'm gonna be in charge. The best part is this. When they get to be four times bigger than I am, and they could squash me in a heartbeat, they still think I'm bigger than they are. It's great. When it comes time to break 'em, it's a whole lot easier. I don't have to work so hard, and it's easier for them, too."

"When I get up on the horse," he continued, "it struggles a bit but mellows out darn fast. Now, my neighbor down the road don't spend much time with his horses until they're big. What a show when he goes to break 'em. They start buckin' and brayin' and carrying on. It's painful to watch."

❤ ❤ ❤

Should we start when our kids are small—playing, setting limits, bonding, and providing discipline? Or should we wait until they are big and try to "break" them later? You know the answer.

Thank you for reading this book. You have just given your children a gift that will last their entire lives—and the lives of their children!

Parents who establish themselves as loving authority figures early in their children's lives create the foundation for a life-long relationship of respect, trust, and love.

Love and Logic Experiment #10

Building Responsibility and Self-Esteem with Chores

Review the steps for Getting Your Kids to Do Chores on pages 157–161.

After reviewing these steps, pick two chores that are appropriate for your child.

Describe each chore to your child and let him or her make a choice.

Start by having your child pick one chore to start with. Why do we suggest giving a choice? Simply because, the odds of your child being cooperative go up when you offer one. If your child doesn't choose within ten seconds flat, make the choice yourself.

Once a chore is chosen, start by working together and having lots of fun.

The goal here is to build positive feelings about helping out around the house. Caution! Focus on your child's effort, avoid criticizing, and focus on the positive.

Gradually shift responsibility onto your child for completing this chore.

Little by little, expect your child to do more and more of the chore without you. Eventually, let your child know that he or she is "big enough" to do the chore alone.

If your child refuses or forgets, do not warn, nag, or remind.

Children need to learn how to complete tasks without their parents standing over them 100% of the time. Children also need to learn how to complete tasks without being nagged, reminded, or warned.

When your child refuses or forgets to do the chore, do it for them. Then say something like, "What a bummer. You forgot to do your chore. I love you too much to nag you, so I did it. How are you planning to pay me for my time?"

Gradually add more chores as your child grows.

Index

Love and Logic Seminars

Jim and Charles Fay, Ph.D. present
"Love and Logic" seminars and personal appearances
for both parents and educators
in many cities each year.

For more information,
contact School Consultant Services at:
1-800-424-3630
or visit our website:
www.loveandlogic.com